Jewish Feasts
and
The Gospel of John

Zacchaeus Studies: New Testament

General Editor: Mary Ann Getty, RSM

Jewish Feasts and The Gospel of John

by

Gale A. Yee

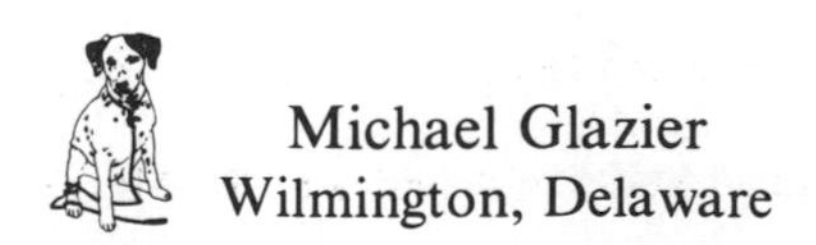

Michael Glazier
Wilmington, Delaware

About the Author

Gale A. Yee did her theological and New Testament studies at Loyola University and did her post-graduate work in theology and Old Testament at St. Michael's College in Toronto, where she received her doctorate. She is a regular contributor to scholarly publications and is presently on the staff of the College of St. Thomas in St. Paul, Minnesota.

First published in 1989 by Michael Glazier, Inc., 1935 West Fourth Street, Wilmington, Delaware 19805.

Library of Congress Cataloging-in-Publication Data

Yee, Gale A., 1949-
Jewish feasts in John's Gospel.

(Zacchaeus studies. New Testament)
1. Bible. N.T. John—Criticism, interpretation, etc.
2. Fasts and feasts in the Bible. 3. Fasts and feasts—Judaism.
I. Title. II. Series.
BS2615.2.Y43 1988 226'.5067 88-82451
ISBN 0-89453-669-9
ISBN: Zacchaeus Studies, NT: 0-89453-662-1

Cover Design by Maureen Daney
Typography by Angela Meades
Printed in the United States of America by St. Mary's Press

Table of Contents

Editor's Note 9

Introduction

Relationship of John to the Synoptics 11

Date and Authorship 12

Literary History 13

Setting of the Evangelist and His Gospel 13

1. The Destruction of the Temple in 70 C.E. 16
2. The Response of the Pharisaic Jewish Community 17
3. The Response of the Johannine Christian Community 21
4. Summary 26

Jewish Feasts and John's Gospel: General Observations 26

"Time" in the Ancient Near East 28

Outline of the Fourth Gospel 29

1. Sabbath

a. Sabbath in the Hebrew Bible and Rabbinic Literature 31

b. Sabbath in John 5:1-47 39

c. Sabbath in John 7:14-24 42

d. Sabbath in John 9:1-41 43

e. Summary 46

2. Passover

a. Passover in the Hebrew Bible 48

b. Passover during the Time of Jesus 57

c. Passover in the Gospel of John: Introduction 59

d. The First Passover: Jn 2:13-25 60

e. The Second Passover: John 6 64

f. The Third Passover: John 13-19 67

3. Tabernacles

a. Tabernacles in the Hebrew Bible 70

b. Tabernacles in the Mishnah 74

c. Tabernacles in the Gospel of John: Introduction 77

d. Tabernacles in John: Before the Feast (Jn 7:1-13) 77

e. Tabernacles in John: The Middle of the Feast (Jn 7:14-36) 78

f. Tabernacles in John: The Last Great Day (Jn 7:37-8:59) 79

g. Tabernacles in John: Conclusion 82

4. Dedication

a. Dedication in 1 and 2 Maccabees 83
b. Dedication in John 10:22-42 88
Select Bibliography 93

Editor's Note

Zacchaeus Studies provide concise, readable and relatively inexpensive scholarly studies on particular aspects of scripture and theology. The New Testament section of the series presents studies dealing with focal or debated questions; and the volumes focus on specific texts of particular themes of current interest in biblical interpretation. Specialists have their professional journals and other forums where they discuss matters of mutual concern, exchange ideas and further contemporary trends of research; and some of their work on contemporary biblical research is now made accessible for students and others in *Zacchaeus Studies.*

The authors in this series share their own scholarship in non-technical language, in the areas of their expertise and interest. These writers stand with the best in current biblical scholarship in the English-speaking world. Since most of them are teachers, they are accustomed to presenting difficult material in comprehensible form without compromising a high level of critical judgment and analysis.

The works of this series are ecumenical in content and purpose and cross credal boundaries. They are designed to augment formal and informal biblical study and discussion. Hopefully they will also serve as texts to enhance and supplement seminary, university and college classes. The series will also aid Bible study groups, adult education and parish religious education classes to develop intelligent, versatile and challenging programs for those they serve.

Mary Ann Getty RSM
New Testament Editor

Introduction

RELATIONSHIP OF JOHN'S GOSPEL TO THE SYNOPTICS

One is struck immediately by the contrasts between the Gospel of John and the Gospels of Matthew, Mark, and Luke, which are generally called the synoptic gospels (Gk. *synopsis* "a seeing together"). The three synoptic gospels present the story of Jesus and the particulars of his ministry in much the same fashion. The extensive agreement in content, vocabulary, style, and arrangement among the three indicates some sort of literary relationship. Of all the possible theories regarding this relationship, the one that is commonly accepted is the so-called Two-Source Theory which posits Mark as the first gospel. According to this theory, Matthew and Luke would have used Mark as a common source, as well as a hypothetical source called Q (German, *Quelle* "source"). Furthermore, they would have enlisted material that was peculiar to their own gospels.

The Gospel of John, however, is markedly different from the Synoptics. For example, while the Synoptics focus on Jesus' ministry in Galilee, John highlights his work in Judea. The Synoptics contain much of Jesus' teaching about the kingdom of God, particularly in the form of parables, while John refers to the kingdom of God only in 3:5 and relates none of Jesus' typical parables. Furthermore, John's gospel contains several extended discourses where Jesus develops themes about who he is, e.g., "I am the bread of life" (6:48), "I am the light of the world" (8:12), "I am the resurrection and the life" (11:25). These familiar discourses are surprisingly not found in the Synoptics. Particularly noteworthy for this study is the divergence between John and the Synoptics regarding chronology. The Synoptics contain only one reference to the Passover celebration which is found in the Passion narratives. During this celebration Jesus is arrested, indicted, and put to death. John, on the contrary, cites three Passover events, portraying Jesus' ministry over a three-year period.

Although the matter has recently been contested,[1] it is fair to say that John's gospel does not have a direct literary dependence upon the Synoptic gospels. John has at his disposal independent traditions about Jesus which had some points of contact with the Synoptic material. These he reworked into his own gospel.

DATE AND AUTHORSHIP

The gospel presumes the destruction of Jerusalem in 70 C.E. as well as the bitter conflicts between the Johannine community and the Jewish synagogue during 80-90 C.E. (see below). The final form most likely took shape between 90-100 C.E., perhaps in Ephesus.

The text identifies its author as "the disciple whom Jesus loved" (Jn 21:20, 24) and an "eyewitness" to the events he describes (19:35). Traditionally, he was thought to be John, son of Zebedee, one of the Twelve who accompanied Jesus. However, the late date of the gospel and its complex literary history (see below) would make this traditional attribution highly improbable. It is more likely that an anonymous evangelist is responsible for the present gospel. His "eyewitness"

[1]See surveys of the literature in Robert Kysar, "The Gospel of John in Current Research," *RelSRev* 9 (1983) 315-316, and in D.A. Carson, "Recent Literature on the Fourth Gospel: Some Reflections," *Themelios* 9 (1983) 10-11.

traditions would be traced back to an equally anonymous disciple of Jesus, the Beloved Disciple, who was not part of the circle of the Twelve.

LITERARY HISTORY

Differences in Greek style in the gospel, the presence of *aporias*, i.e., inconsistencies or breaks in the text, and repetitions in the discourses, reveal that the present gospel was not composed at one sitting by a single author. Rather, it is a product of a complex literary history, but the exact nature of this history continues to be discussed. As we have said, the evangelist had access to different sources from which he created his work. One of the most influential theories investigating the particular character of John's sources is that of Rudolph Bultmann. According to Bultmann, three sources can be detected in the fourth gospel: a sign source, a discourse source, and a passion narrative. Bultmann's theory continues to be modified and refined.

Furthermore, besides the sources that the evangelist used and the transformation of these sources in the preaching and teaching of the Johannine community, the evangelist's own composition underwent editorial activity by a later redactor who anonymously contributed to the final form of the gospel. This redactor may have been a disciple in the Johannine community in which the evangelist lived and whose needs he addressed.

SETTING OF THE EVANGELIST AND HIS GOSPEL

We now turn to the important matter of the setting of the evangelist and his community. An informed understanding of the historical situation during which John wrote not only assists us in discerning John's theology regarding Jewish feasts, but also has wider hermeneutical implications. Of all the gospels and even the rest of the New Testament itself, John's gospel is noteworthy in its vitriolic anti-Jewish pole-mic.[2] Its anti-Semitic potential has been held culpable for providing a canonical foundation that encouraged and supported Christian anti-Semitism from the second century C.E. to the present day.[3]

In contrast to the Synoptics where there are sixteen instances of the term, "the Jews," John's gospel cites about seventy references to "the Jews." The first and lasting impression that the term conveys is disbelief and hostility towards Jesus. "The Jews" misunderstand Jesus (6:52; 7:35; 8:22). Like their ancestors against Moses, they murmur against Jesus (6:41). They persecute and seek to kill him (5:16-18; 7:1; 8:59; 10:31). They are no longer children of Abraham, the father of their own people, but rather children of the father of lies, the devil himself (8:34-47). In contrast to the Synoptics where the Jewish religious leaders and the ambiguous "crowd" or "people" demand Jesus' death (Mt 27:20-23; Mk 15:11-13; Lk 23:13-23), in John *the Jews* cry out, "Away with him, away with him, crucify him!" (Jn 12:14-15).

The key question is the actual identity of these Jews in the intent of the evangelist. Exegetical studies reveal that John's use of the designation, "the Jews," is inconsistent. Sometimes the word is used neutrally to explain Jewish religious customs (2:6, 19:40) or refer to their feasts (2:13; 5:1; 6:4). However, in many cases the evangelist does intend the term to mean the opponents of Jesus, but exactly "who these opponents

[2]We distinguish between the terms "anti-Jewish" and "anti-Semitic." Anti-Jewishness rejects Judaism on theological grounds as a nonviable way to salvation. Anti-semitism, on the other hand, rejects the Jews on racial and ethnic grounds. See Edward H. Flanner, "Anti-Judaism and Anti-Semitism: A Necessary Distinction," *JES* 10 (1973) 582-583.

[3]Consult in particular Eldon Jay Epp, "Anti-Semitism and the Popularity of the Fourth Gospel in Christianity," *Central Conference of American Rabbis Journal* 22 (1975) 35-57; Janis E. Leibig, "John and 'the Jews': Theological Antisemitism in the Fourth Gospel," *JES* 20 (1983) 209-234; John T. Townsend, "The Gospel of John and the Jews: The Story of a Religious Divorce," *AntiSemitism and the Foundations of Christianity*, Alan T. Davies, ed. (New York: Paulist, 1979) 72-97; John Koenig, "John: A Painful Break With Judaism," *Jews and Christians in Dialogue: New Testament Foundations* (Philadelphia: Westminster, 1979) 122-136; Reginald Fuller, "The 'Jews' in the Fourth Gospel," *Dialog* 16 (1977) 31-37; Mary Ann Getty, "The Jews and John's Passion Narrative," *Liturgy* 22 (1977) 6-10.

are?" is another question. For some exegetes, "the Jews" does not simply represent the Jewish people, but is John's symbol of the sinful disbelieving world. For others, the hostile connotation does not signify all Jews, but a smaller group within the nation, such as the religious leaders, or the Judeans, those who live in the geographical area of Judea.

Whatever meaning the evangelist intended by the designation, "the Jews," one also needs to consider the comprehensive effect of the term, particularly on a Gentile-Christian audience from the second century onward. In contrast to the Synoptics, John does not make the fine distinctions between religious authorities and the people in his use of the phrase. Moreover, the expression obfuscates the plurality that existed within Jewish society itself during Jesus' time by presenting such a monolithic picture of Judaism. No longer does one have the rich and poor, sinners and righteous, Sadducees, Herodians, Zealots, scribes, elders, tax-collectors, prostitutes. All are lumped together in the term, "the Jews." For John, the Jewish people stereotypically epitomizes all that is evil in its rejection of Christ. As John ignores such fine distinctions, so too is the uninformed Gentile Christian reader in danger of typecasting the Jews.

According to Epp,

> ...when a reader has finished all twenty-one chapters of John's gospel, the term "the Jews" has been heated by the fire of narrative controversy between Jesus and "the Jews," has been hammered by its vehement repetition, and has been forged by the bitter and hostile contexts of many of its occurrences into a red-hot spear, which not only has pierced the side of the Lord of the Church but now seems menacing also to the Gentile reader of this Christian account of the Gospel.[4]

One receives the impression from John that Jesus the Jew is no longer part of his own people. Rather, Jesus denounces

[4]Epp, "Anti-Semitism," 41. Cf. also, Leibig, "John and 'the Jews,'" 214-216.

them for their lack of understanding and their rejection. Tragically, the condemnation of the Johannine Jesus has given warrant to the persecution of Jesus' own people by Christians down through the centuries.

The anti-Jewishness of John's gospel is particularly relevant for our study of Jewish feasts and John's gospel. As we will see, John's gospel proclaims a replacement theology: The person and work of Jesus supersedes Jewish liturgical celebrations and causes them to become obsolete. It is no small wonder that the most intense Christian pogroms against the Jews occurred through the centuries during their religious feasts, particularly Passover. These feasts, however, continue tenaciously to be celebrated by the Jewish people. They were not abolished with the appearance of Jesus. It is incumbent upon Christians to recognize their validity and legitimacy as authentic worship of God.

It becomes crucial, therefore, to understand the reasons behind John's portrayal of "the Jews." To what extent do historical circumstances compel the evangelist to depict the Jews so antagonistically? We see three factors coming into play in the formation of the Johannine picture of "the Jews":

1) the destruction of the temple in 70 C.E.,
2) the Pharisaic Jewish response to this event and to the phenomenon of Christianity, and
3) the Johannine Christian response in the post-70 period and counter-response to Judaism.

We will take each of these in turn.

1) The Destruction of the Temple in 70 C.E.

The destruction of the second temple and the city of Jerusalem by the Romans in 70 C.E. was a tragic event that left its mark on the life and worship of the Jewish people from that point onward. The temple symbolized God's presence with the people. It was the home of an elaborate system of priests and cultic personnel who oversaw the countless animal sacrifices offered in worship to God. As God's holy dwelling, it was the center of the people's piety.

To account for the destruction of the first temple in 587 B.C.E., the Deuteronomistic Historian charged Israel with the idolatry so characteristic of the preexilic period (cf. 1 Kings 9:6-8). When the people abandoned God in running after false idols, so did God forsake the people. This divine renunciation of the people was symbolized in the razing of the first temple. However, having undergone the fires of the exile and then being restored back to the land, the Jews believed that the construction of the second temple signified their reconciliation with God.

Hence, the destruction of the temple for the second time precipitated a theological crisis of profound proportions. The Jews struggled to understand precisely what this event meant regarding their relationship with God. There were four interrelated social and religious problems that needed to be dealt with. First of all, how does one explain the disaster of the temple's destruction for the second time? Secondly, how does one now achieve atonement without the temple cult, its priesthood, and its animal sacrifices? Thirdly, how does one now cope with this new age? How does one create a way of life on a new basis entirely? Fourthly, how does one account for the new social forms that emerge upon the collapse of the old social structure?

Although there were other responses to the disaster, we will focus on two: the Pharisaic Jewish response and the response of the Johannine Christian community. It is the conflict between these two communities in their struggle for self-definition and identity, particularly in the post-70 period, that is reflected in John's Gospel and its theology of the Jewish feasts.

2) The Response of the Pharisaic Jewish Community

After 70 C.E. the Pharisees emerged as the dominant religious sect in Judaism. They are important for our study not only because the gospels depict them as the principal opponents of Jesus, but also because Judaism as we know it today traces its roots back to the great Pharisaic rabbis. It was the efforts of these rabbis that carried the Jewish people through the traumatic post-70 period.[5]

Unlike other Jewish sects e.g. the Sadducees, Zealots, or the Essenes, the Pharisees were much better equipped to deal with the post-70 disaster. First of all, they advanced a comprehensive program for Jewish religious life to replace the temple sacrificial system. Secondly, their doctrines of providence, life after death, retribution, and recompense for suffering helped the people to deal with the catastrophe of 70 C.E. Thirdly, their hermeneutical principles allowed them the flexibility to adapt ancient laws and traditions to fit changing circumstances. Fourth and fifth, they enjoyed the confidence not only of the Romans, but also large sectors of the Jewish population. Sixth, they vigorously asserted their claims as the single legitimate authority in Judaism, vis-à-vis the other weakened Jewish parties. Their theology and interpretation of tradition came to represent "normative Judaism" in the post-70 era.

Under Rabbi Yoḥanan ben Zakkai (ca. 1-80 C.E.), the Pharisees moved their headquarters from the ruins of the city of Jerusalem to Jabneh (Jamnia). Jabneh was located on the coastal plain south of Joppa. According to 2 Chron 26:6, Jabneh was once a Philistine stronghold that was conquered by Uzziah, king of Judah, in the eighth century B.C.E. Yoḥanan ben Zakkai responded to the theological challenge of the fall of the temple and Jerusalem with inspiring wisdom and faith. He initiated and implemented a program that was not only intended to heal the soul of the people, but also reconstruct their social, political, and religious life from the ashes of Roman desolation. His paramount concern was instilling a renewed sense of identity into a people close to despair and dissolution.

[5]See Jacob Neusner, *First-Century Judaism in Crisis: Johanan ben Zakkai and the Renaissance of Torah* (Nashville: Abingdon Press, 1975) and W.D. Davies, *The Setting of the Sermon on the Mount* (Cambridge: University Press, 1966) 256-315, for broader treatments of the discussion that follows.

Two centuries earlier Rabbi Simeon the Righteous taught: "On three things does the age stand: on the Torah, on the Temple service, and on acts of piety." In view of the temple's destruction, these three things needed reinterpretation for Rabbi Yoḥanan. The temple was traditionally the place where the iniquities of Israel were atoned for through the sacrifices of animals by the priests. Meditating on Hos 6:6, "For I desire mercy (*ḥ*esed), not sacrifice," Rabbi Yoḥanan saw that acts of *ḥesed*, or mercy and compassion, now effect one's atonement with God. The means toward atonement was switched from the temple precincts to the Jewish hearth and home. Under Pharisaic leadership, all Jews equally were called to be priests offering sacrifices to God in acts of compassion.

Moreover, with the temple's destruction an increased emphasis on Torah came to the fore. It was at Jabneh that the final codification of the Hebrew biblical canon occurred. Torah included not only intensive study of the written Torah, but also of the oral Torah as interpreted by the Pharisees. The synagogue became the natural locus for this study, emerging as the major center of Jewish religious life with the temple's end. Many of the customs and rituals of the temple were deliberately transferred to the synagogue.

Acts of piety, the third aspect of Jewish life, involved not only obedience to God's commandments and statutes, but also their execution in an attitude of love and mercy. Rabbi Yoḥanan thus highlighted the internal moral posture of the Jew before God as it was manifested in these external acts.

Judaism in the post-70 era would now continue on the foundation of intensive Torah study, doing God's commandments, and especially performing acts of mercy and compassion. Under Rabbi Yoḥanan, Jabneh became for Judaism the center of halakic learning, as well as the focal point of religious and political administration in place of the destroyed Jerusalem.

Particularly important for this study is that the most immediate and pressing problems that Rabbi Yoḥanan had to deal with were in the area of liturgy. Holy days and festivals, formerly observed mainly in the temple, now had to be adapted to fit the needs of a post-temple community. Rabbi Yoḥanan assumed the authority, previously reserved for the temple priesthood, to fix a proper liturgical calendar. He issued a series of decrees on a variety of liturgical legislation, e.g., the time and place of the blowing of the *shofar*, the observance of Passover, Tabernacles, Sabbath, and New Moon celebrations that were previously dependent on the temple rituals. In all this legislation, Rabbi Yoḥanan desired not a substitute for the temple and its practices, but a valid equivalent to the temple. This equivalent would be the synagogue with the Pharisees as its legitimate overseers.

In adjudicating over liturgical matters, Rabbi Yoḥanan's assumption of authority vis-à-vis the priesthood was not without conflict. Although displaced from the temple and considerably weakened, some priests and temple officials survived the catastrophe and sought assiduously to reclaim their authority. Several of Yoḥanan's ordinances stripped the priests of their privileges and transferred them to the Pharisees. This strategy for Pharisaic legitimation inevitably brought him into conflict with the priests who challenged the growing influence of the Pharisees. The priests were not willing to surrender so easily their powers that were founded on ancient hereditary succession. Moreover, they were fearful that the new Torah-based renewal program would divert the people's energies from rebuilding the temple and restoring their former priestly prerogatives.

The situation of the Pharisees was further compounded by the deep divisions among the Pharisees themselves. These divisions can be traced back to the great pre-70 Pharisaic Houses of Hillel and Shammai. The House of Hillel, of which Rabbi Yoḥanan was a disciple, took a more liberal stand on the interpretation of the Law and adaptations to new circumstances. The House of Shammai favored a more conservative approach. Hence, the Pharisees had to cope with establishing unity among their own ranks, as well as bringing about unity among a fragmented people.

We see then that the state of Judaism in the crisis of 70

C.E. and its aftermath was quite complex. The Jewish community struggled to find equilibrium in making a transition to a new way of life. The question at stake was the identity of Judaism bereft of its temple. The liturgical feasts of the temple and the piety of the people were in a state of transition and adaptation. The old order and way of life having gone for the most part, the new order under the Pharisees labored and strained to find authority and acceptance in the wider Jewish community.

3) The Response of the Johannine Christian Community

We now turn to a discussion of the Johannine community's response to the destruction of the temple and the calamitous post-70 era. Like the Jewish community, the Johannine community itself was undergoing an evolution. The Johannine scholar, Raymond Brown, observes a four-stage development in the history of the community.[6]

Phase One would cover the period from the mid-50's to late 80's C.E. The community was first composed of Jews who accepted Jesus as the Davidic messiah and had a lower Christology, i.e., an understanding of Jesus that did not imply divinity. A second group of Jews who had an anti-temple bias and were influenced by their Samaritan converts joined the original group. This group catalyzed the development of a higher, preexistent Christology. This Christology, which implied divinity for Jesus, led to controversy with the Jews and to their expulsion from the synagogue. Their bitter conflict with the Jewish community forged their inimical understanding of "the Jews." In their alienation, the Johannine community no longer saw itself as Jewish.

Phase Two reflects the period during which the Gospel was written, ca. 90 C.E. With its high Christology, the community consolidated its understanding and identity not only over and against the "Jews," but also several other groups:

[6]See Raymond E. Brown, *The Community of the Beloved Disciple* (New York: Paulist, 1979).

the followers of John the Baptist, the Jewish Christians who remained in the synagogue, the Jewish Christians of inadequate faith, and Apostolic Christians.

A split within the Johannine community over several doctrinal matters (ca. 100 C.E.) characterizes Phase Three. The division occasions the writing of the Johannine epistles during this period. Phase Four covers the final separation of the community into orthodox and gnostic camps during the second century C.E.

At this point, we are concerned primarily with Phase One, the pre-gospel period of the community and its relationship with the Jewish community. Phase One correlates with the time up to the destruction of the temple and the earlier years of the Pharisees at Jabneh. Undoubtedly, the decisions at Jabneh regarding liturgy, synagogue, and the formation of the canon affected this Jewish Christian community, as well as the claims of other Jewish groups.

The high Christology (an anathema to Jewish sensibilities), the opposition to the temple and its cult, and the presence of Samaritan converts that characterized the later developments of Phase One all made the Johannine Jewish Christian community particularly threatening in the eyes of Jews, who were in a fluctuating and unpredictable stage of transition themselves. It was during this phase that the Johannine community considered itself completely divorced from the Jewish people. It saw this divorce in its "expulsion from the synagogue," the surrogate of temple piety for both camps.

In his famous investigation of the Fourth Gospel, J. Louis Martyn deals specifically with John 9:22 which reads in part:

> For the Jews had already agreed that if any one should confess him to be the Christ, he was to be *put out of the synagogue.* (Cf. John 12:42; 16:2)

According to Martyn, the historical background to John 9:22 was the *Birkat ha-Minim* ("blessing against heretics"), which he believes was an official Jewish decision against Jewish Christians designed to identify and then excommunicate them from the synagogue. A suspected Jewish Christian would be asked to lead the congregation. If he faltered when reading the twelfth Benediction, he was removed from the synagogue.[7]

Martyn's hypothesis needs to be qualified in order that we may understand more clearly the bitter animosity between the Johannine community and "the Jews." The *Birkat ha-Minim* was the twelfth blessing added to the synagogue prayer, the *Shemoneh Esreh* (The Eighteen Benedictions). According to the Babylonian Talmud (*b. Ber.* 28b-29a), Rabbi Yoḥanan's successor at Jabneh, Rabbi Gamaliel II, commissioned a prayer ca. 85-95 C.E. against the growing number of heretics (*minim*) that afflicted the Jewish community. Such a measure was aimed at unifying Judaism along clearer Pharisaic lines during the post-temple period.

The question, however, is the exact identity of the *minim* in the original version of the blessing for the Jabnean rabbis. In 1898, Solomon Schecter discovered a rendition of the blessing at the Cairo Genizah which reads:

> For apostates (*meshumaddim*) let there be no hope, and the dominion of arrogance mayest Thou speedily root out in our days; and let Christians (*ha-Notzrim*) and *minim* perish in a moment, let them be blotted out of the book of the living and let them not be written with the righteous.

The problem with Martyn's hypothesis is that he accepts as the original Jabnean formulation the Genizah version that specifies Christians among the *minim.* Recent studies however strongly question that the Genizah version of the *Birkat ha-Minim* was the original Jabnean promulgation and that the malediction's *principal* target was the Jewish Christian sector.[8] "Heretics" meant more than Jewish Christianity for

[7]J. Louis Martyn, *History and Theology in the Fourth Gospel* (2nd ed.; Nashville: Abingdon, 1979) 50-62.

[8]Steven T. Katz, "Issues in the Separation of Judaism and Christianity after 70 C.E.: A Reconsideration," *JBL* 103 (1984) 63-76; Reuven Kimelman, "*Birkat Ha-*

the Jabnean rabbis. During this time of Pharisaic struggle for authority and legitimation, the "*minim*" were all who deviated from Pharisaic norms; not only Jewish Christians, but also Jewish gnostics, apocalypticists, Hellenizers, Essenes, and probably Sadducees.

The *Birkat ha-Minim* was more a means of self-defense to reduce any threat to the surviving Jewish community, than a direct act of aggression against Jewish Christians. It functioned as a filter, not an excommunicatory ban, that made it very uncomfortable for heretics to participate in the synagogue, which was slowly but surely becoming the temple's replacement. The intent was the gradual withdrawal of heretics (which included, but not uniquely, Jewish Christians) from the Jewish community. The purpose of the act was primarily intramural: to conform post-70 Judaism which was in danger of disintegration to the policies of the Pharisees, the ascendant power group. Principally an act of Pharisaic self-definition and self-defense, it also set criteria for the exclusion of those who did not harmonize with this definition.

One needs to keep in mind this self-defining function of the *Birkat ha-Minim* and that it was meant for a wider population than just the Jewish Christians. From a hermeneutical point of view, this is particularly the case when evaluating the anti-Jewishness of the Fourth Gospel. Sensing animosity against themselves, the Johannine Jewish Christians, who were also struggling for self-definition and identity like the Jews, would regard the *Birkat ha-Minim* as tantamount to an assault directed solely against *them* to "expel them from the synagogue." Representing the community, John would write as if a Jewish policy of excommunication was in effect against them explicitly.

In any crisis situation, the group that perceives itself to be threatened will close ranks and focus all energy on "the

Minim and the Lack of Evidence for an Anti-Christian Jewish Prayer in Late Antiquity," *Jewish and Christian Self-Definition: Vol. 2 Aspects of Judaism in the Greco-Roman Period*, E.P. Sanders, ed. (Philadelphia: Fortress, 1981) 226-244.

enemy." This was the case for the Jewish community; it was the case also for the Johannine community which was keenly aware of its minority status within the larger Jewish society. This minority status would make it overly sensitive to any change in the synagogue liturgy. The Johannine community had integrated its belief in Jesus with its usual worship in the synagogue. This assimilation into the synagogue, however, was not without tension. On one hand, the synagogue liturgy itself was in flux in its continual adaptation to the post-temple period. On the other hand, the high Christology of the Johannine community alienated the Jews of the synagogue. The Johannine sense of exclusion from the synagogue brought this tension to a head, creating a theological crisis not unlike the Jews' own crisis in their loss of the temple.

Several factors combined, then, to contribute to the Johannine alienation from the larger Jewish population: on the one side, a sense of inferiority arising from a minority position, a perception that a liturgical change singled out them alone, and a developing higher Christology that was offensive to the Jews; on the other side, a community traumatized by the destruction of its temple and struggling for stability, a liturgy that was evolving from temple to synagogue worship, and the defensive posture of Pharisaic Judaism striving for legitimate authority.

When the Johannine community felt that it was cut off from the synagogue, the very locus of its piety at the time, the connection with the Jewish community itself was severed and was replaced by much hurt and bitterness. Its redefinition apart from the synagogue would now be conceived antagonistically in terms of the paradigm "in distinction from," rather than "in connection with." The community that once saw itself as Jewish now no longer does so. Instead, "the Jews" would now represent all that was inimical to Johannine self-definition. As the *minim* represented all who deviated from Pharisaic norms, "the Jews" symbolized all who rejected Jesus according to Johannine norms. Moreover, to intensify its self-definition, "in distinction from," the Johannine Jesus now nullified and replaced all the Jewish liturgical institutions that the community lost in its divorce from the synagogue: Sabbath, Passover, Tabernacles, and Dedication.

4) Summary

A proper understanding of the setting of the evangelist and his community is essential in interpreting the Fourth Gospel. The anti-Jewishness of the gospel is influenced by a number of factors that involve the emerging self-definition of two different groups that clashed during a period of crisis. The first group, Pharisaic Judaism, suffered the destruction of its temple by the Romans and the resultant disunity of the Jewish people. The threat of the people's extinction motivated Pharisaic Judaism on a course of action that not only helped the people's recovery, but also brought it in conflict with special interest groups within Judaism. One of these groups was Johannine Christianity. The Johannine Jewish Christians also had to deal with the loss of the temple and the liturgical transition to the synagogue. Their evolving higher Christology, however, estranged them from the community of which it once was a part. Both groups strove for authenticity, recognition, and legitimacy. Tragically, however, both groups will define themselves over and against each other as conflict deepens between them.

JEWISH FEASTS AND JOHN'S GOSPEL: GENERAL OBSERVATIONS

In the previous section we tried to show that the interpretation of John's gospel must be viewed in context of the historical situation of the evangelist and his community. The conflicts in the post-70 era between the Johannine community and the Jewish authorities, viz., the Pharisees, are transposed back into the ministry of the historical Jesus. The Synoptics also paint a picture of Jesus coming head to head with the Pharisees. However, it is in John's gospel that these opponents are bitterly focused into the term "the Jews." Perceiving their "exclusion from the synagogue," the Johannine community no longer felt a solidarity with the Jewish people.

Wayne Meeks astutely points out that "the Fourth Gospel is most anti-Jewish just at the points it is most Jewish."[9] This is particularly the case where the evangelist links Jesus' signs and discourses with Jewish feasts. The Synoptics mention only one Jewish feast, viz., Passover, and then only in connection with the Passion narrative. However, John relates the story of the cleansing of the temple *early on* in Jesus' ministry during the time of Passover (Jn 2:13-23). In contrast to the Synoptics, he situates the Sabbath controversy in the context of an unnamed "feast of the Jews" (Jn 5:1). He alone specifies the feast of Tabernacles (Jn 7:2) and Dedication (Jn 10:22), as well as returning to the feast of Passover at the end of Jesus' earthly ministry. The attention that John gives these festivals strongly suggests that these feasts had an important place in the piety of his community as *Jewish* Christians.

We see a parallel development to the Pharisaic adaptation from temple to synagogue in the post-70 period in John's reinterpretation of the Jewish feasts. Just as the Pharisees under Yoḥanan ben Zakkai respond to the destruction of the temple by adapting its liturgical feasts to the synagogue, so does John respond to the loss of the synagogue by reinterpreting the Jewish liturgical calendar in light of the person Jesus. Sadly, the model of self-definition behind both these adaptations is formulated in terms of "in distinction from." In the case of Pharisaic Judaism, liturgical changes are made "in distinction from" the *minim* (heretics), which included Jewish Christianity. In the case of John and the Johannine community, reinterpretation of the Jewish liturgical calendar is made "in distinction from" the Jewish community. For John, Jesus replaces and abrogates the traditional feasts of the Jews.

[9]Wayne A. Meeks, "'Am I a Jew?'—Johannine Christianity and Judaism," *Christianity, Judaism and Other Greco-Roman Cults: Part One*, Jacob Neusner, ed. (Leiden: Brill, 1975) 172.

"TIME" IN THE ANCIENT NEAR EAST

Before we begin our discussion of the Jewish feasts and their reinterpretation by the Fourth Evangelist, we turn to the matter of "time" in the Ancient Near East. To appreciate the Jewish festivals one must be aware of ancient near eastern divisions of time, since the feasts occur at specified periods of the Jewish year. The history of ancient near eastern calendars is quite complex, but we are able to make a few observations about the Jewish liturgical year.

Time in the Ancient Near East was measured by the courses of two major celestial bodies: the sun and the moon. The calendar day was measured by the passage of the sun and, unlike our reckoning, began in the evening. The Jewish week consisted of the familiar seven days, the seventh being the Sabbath, the day of rest.

The calendar year was primarily a lunar one. The waxing and waning of the moon was a cycle of about twenty-nine or so days constituting a month. The twelve month lunar year was approximately eleven days shorter than the solar year of 365 days. The names of the twelve months were adopted from the Babylonian calendar, although their older Canaanite designations do appear in the Hebrew Bible. For example, Dt 16:1 stipulates that the feast of Passover must be celebrated in the month of Abib, Nisan in the Babylonian calendar. The following outlines the months of the Jewish year and their approximate correlations with our modern-day calendar:

I.	Nisan	March-April
II.	Iyyar	April-May
III.	Sivan	May-June
IV.	Tammuz	June-July
V.	Ab	July-August
VI.	Elul	August-September
VII.	Tishri	September-October
VIII.	Marheshvan	October-November
IX.	Kislev	November-December

X.	Tebeth	December-January
XI.	Shebat	January-February
XII.	Adar	February-March

As it stands here, the beginning of the year would occur in the spring in the month of Nisan. However, the two oldest liturgical calendars in the Hebrew Bible, Ex 23:14-17 and 34:18-23, both presuppose a year that once began in autumn. The exact date when the new year was fixed in the spring is not certain. It may have been around the time of the Babylonian occupation of Palestine in the sixth century B.C.E. The rabbis will handle the calendar inconsistencies regarding the new year by positing four "New Year" days. On the 1st of Nisan is the New Year for kings and feasts; on the 1st of Elul is the New Year for the tithe on cattle; on the 1st of Tishri is the New Year for the years of foreign kings, the sabbatical years, Jubilee years; and the 1st of Shebat is the New Year for fruit trees (*m. Roš. Haš.* 1:1).

OUTLINE OF THE FOURTH GOSPEL

Scholars envision the overall structure of John's Gospel differently. We follow Raymond Brown's general outline of the gospel primarily because his structure highlights Jesus' activities during the principal feasts of the Jews.[10] Brown divides the book into four major parts: the Prologue, the Book of Signs, the Book of Glory, and the Epilogue.

The very familiar Prologue was an early Christian hymn that probably originated in the Johannine community. It introduces us to the preexistent Word who becomes incarnate, making his dwelling among humanity. The Book of Signs describes Jesus' public ministry. Unlike the Synoptics, John focuses only on seven miracles of Jesus which function as "signs" to the people that Jesus is the Father's own reve-

[10]Raymond E. Brown, S.S., *The Gospel According to John (i-xii)* (Garden City: Doubleday, 1966) cxxxviii-cxliv.

lation. The majority of Jews will reject Jesus. In the Book of Glory, however, Jesus will reveal his glory to those who believe in the "hour" of his crucifixion, resurrection, and ascension. The Epilogue balances the Prologue with the story of Jesus' post-resurrection appearances in Galilee.

John situates certain events in Jesus' ministry specifically during four Jewish festival seasons: Sabbath, Passover, Tabernacles, and Dedication. According to John, Jesus replaces these feasts in his special relationship to the Father, making them obsolete. The Book of Signs is important for this study because it is here that John explores the significance of Jesus in light of the symbolism of the Jewish feasts. He will, however, repeat the festal themes in the Book of Glory, particularly in the Passion Narrative. We will therefore focus our discussion predominately on the Book of Signs, pointing out in the course of our study where the festival motifs are resumed in the Book of Glory.

The following is an outline of John's Gospel with special attention to the Book of Signs:

I. THE PROLOGUE: John 1:1-18
II. THE BOOK OF SIGNS: John 1:19—12:50
   A. The Beginning of Jesus' Revelation (Jn 1:19-51)
   B. From Cana to Cana—Jesus manifests his glory in various ways, in various places, eliciting various responses (John 2-4)
   C. Jesus and the Jewish Feasts (John 5-10)
      1. Sabbath (Jn 5:1-47. Also 7:14-24; 9:1-41)
      2. Passover (Jn 6:1-71. Also 2:13-25; John 13—19)
      3. Tabernacles (Jn 7:1—8:59)
      4. Dedication (Jn 10:22-39)
   D. Passover Season—Jesus moves toward his hour of death and glory (John 11—12)
III. THE BOOK OF GLORY: John 13:1—20:31
IV. THE EPILOGUE: John 21:1-25

1

Sabbath

a. Sabbath in the Hebrew Bible and Rabbinic Literature

Scholars have sought the origins of Sabbath in a number of different places, such as among the Babylonians, the Canaanites, or the Kenites.[11] It was the Hebrews, however, who vested the seventh day of the week with a particular religious significance. The noun *šabbat* is derived from the root *šbt* which means "to cease or stop (work), rest." Although we will see these motives operative, it was not simply for humanitarian reasons that the people refrained from work on this day. Rather, it was because the Sabbath was a sign of God's covenant with the people. The day was made *holy* by God and Israel was charged to keep that day so.

The practice of keeping the Sabbath was quite early in Israel. One finds ancient injunctions regarding the Sabbath in the two versions of the Decalogue: Ex 20:8-11 and Dt 5:12-15. These versions contain two different traditions that explain why the Sabbath was a day of rest. The Sabbath command in the original form of the Decalogue probably did not contain an accompanying theological rationale. Redactors representing two spheres of thought on the

[11]For a thorough discussion of Sabbath and its traditions, consult the essays in Kenneth A. Strand, ed., *The Sabbath in Scripture and History* (Washington: Review and Herald Publishing Association, 1982).

Sabbath added the explanations later. Both interpretations are quite illuminating regarding the significance of the observance. As a springboard to our discussion, we will compare the two texts in the following highlighting the differences in *italics*:

Ex 20:8-11

"*Remember* the sabbath day, to keep it holy. Six days you shall labor, and do all your work; but the seventh day is a sabbath to the Lord your God; in it you shall not do any work, you, or your son, or your daughter, your manservant, or your maidservant, or your cattle, or the sojourner who is within your gates; *for in six days the Lord made heaven and earth, the sea, and all that is in them, and rested the seventh day; therefore the Lord blessed the sabbath day and hallowed it.*"

Dt. 5:12-15

"*Observe* the sabbath day, to keep it holy, *as the Lord your God commanded you.* Six days you shall labor, and do all your work; but the seventh day is a sabbath to the Lord your God; in it you shall not do any work, you, or your son, or your daughter, or your manservant, or your maidservant, *or your ox, or your ass*, or *any of* your cattle, or the sojourner who is within your gates, *that your manservant and your maidservant may rest as well as you. You shall remember that you were a servant in the land of Egypt, and the Lord your God brought you out thence with a mighty hand and an outstretched arm; therefore the Lord your God commanded you to keep the sabbath day.*"

The explanation in Ex 20:11 of the Decalogue grounds the Sabbath in the creative work of God. The text recalls the Priestly account of creation in Genesis 1, an account that begins with light on the first day and culminates in the creation of humanity on the sixth day (Gen 1:3-27). The conclusion of the story reads:

> And on the seventh day God finished his work which he had done, and he rested on the seventh day from all his work which he had done. So God blessed the seventh day and hallowed it, because on it God rested from all his work which he had done in creation. (Gen 2:2-3)

Gazing upon all that he had fashioned with joy and satisfaction, God declared it "very good" (Gen 1:31). Then, in a rare instance of anthropomorphism by the Priestly writer, God rested from his labors. The text goes on to state that God blessed the seventh day and made it holy. The Hebrew idea of what is *qdš* "holy" entails "separation." God separates the seventh day from the other days of the week, thereby making it a holy day dedicated to God.

According to Lev 23:1-3, the holiness of the day places Sabbath among the other appointed feasts of God, such as Passover, Unleavened Bread, and Tabernacles, although in contrast to these yearly feasts the celebration of the Sabbath is weekly. The negative aspect of refraining from work also has a positive feature. It allows a special time to worship God as a people. It becomes a weekly "holy convocation" unto the Lord. When is it to be held on the seventh day? In Lev 23:32 we read, "from evening to evening shall you keep your sabbath."

Since God made the day holy, the Israelite is called, as an individual and a member of a people, to keep the day holy. Just as God rested from all that he had made on the seventh day, so too does the obedient Israelite imitate God and do the same. According to Ex 20:8, the Israelite is exhorted in worship to "remember *(zākôr)*" the Sabbath. Not simply an intellectual recalling, the Hebrew concept of "remembrance" signified that what was remembered of the past was "made present" or "relived" liturgically. Hence, to remember the Sabbath was to participate again in the creative work of God and be recreated anew. It meant looking back on one's own week's work, pronouncing it "very good," and pausing for refreshment and renewal.

Another Priestly text gives us further insight on the Sabbath:

> Six days shall work be done, but the seventh day is a sabbath of solemn rest, holy to the Lord; whoever does any work on the sabbath day shall be put to death. Therefore the people of Israel shall keep the sabbath, observing the sabbath throughout their generations, as a perpetual covenant. It is a sign for ever between me and the people of Israel that in six days the Lord made heaven and earth, and on the seventh day he rested, and was refreshed. (Ex 31:15-17)

The theme of the Sabbath's holiness is recapitulated here. The death penalty emphasizes the seriousness of its observance for anyone who disobeys it and does work. Noteworthy is the Priestly motif that Sabbath is a "sign" of God's "perpetual covenant" with the people.[12] The Sabbath becomes the visible symbol of God's enduring relationship with Israel, a covenantal relationship that began at the time of creation itself. It is a reminder of the first Sabbath when God's very self rested and was refreshed after creating the world.

Complementing Ex 20:8-11, the Decalogue injunction in Dt 5:12-15 features other aspects of the Sabbath. First of all, the Sabbath is observed for humanitarian reasons: so that one's male and female servants and one's beasts of burden would also have the opportunity to rest from their labors. Nevertheless, the command advances beyond the humani-

[12]See the Priestly account of the flood story in Gen 9:8-17 where the rainbow is the sign of God's covenant with Noah. Cf. also Ezek 20:12, 20 regarding Sabbath as a sign.

tarian argument to a theological one:

> You shall remember that you were a servant in the land of Egypt, and the Lord your God brought you out thence with a mighty hand and an outstretched arm; therefore the Lord your God commanded you to keep the sabbath day. (Dt. 5:15)

Dt 5:12-15 grounds the Sabbath in God's dramatic liberation of Israel from slavery in Egypt. Every week the Israelites are called to "remember" or "make present again" the time when they were once slaves, a people who were in bondage and were delivered therefrom. Remembering the past makes them cognizant of the present: that within their own household are those of an inferior social status. These too need refreshment and rejuvenation. Moreover, revealed in the Sabbath command is a glimpse of the future, when God will abolish social inequalities creating a free people worshipping him.

The two traditions preserved in the Hebrew Bible—one founding Sabbath on God's creation, the other on God's liberation—are by no means mutually exclusive. Both emphasize the tremendous works God has done for the people. The creation of the world and humanity was God's first act in his history of salvation. God's liberation of the Israelites from Egypt was another spectacular moment in this history. Both are recalled weekly by each Israelite in the Sabbath observance. God's creative work is redemptive; God's liberating work is creative. In a posture of worship at each Sabbath celebration, one acclaims God as both Creator and Redeemer (Re-creator) in covenant with the people of Israel.

During the Babylonian Exile after the destruction of the first temple, the Sabbath took on a new significance as a sign of the covenant. This significance is particularly seen in the Priestly texts, written during the Exile, cited above. The celebration of Sabbath did not need a temple in order to be observed. One need only to set aside the seventh day as a day consecrated to God.

Having looked at the theology of Sabbath, we turn our

attention to the matter of "keeping" the Sabbath. What exactly is involved in keeping the Sabbath holy? Some activities that are specifically prohibited in the Hebrew Bible are baking or boiling food (Ex 16:23), activities associated with the plowing and harvesting seasons (Ex 34:21), lighting fires (Ex 35:3), gathering sticks (Num 15:32), conducting any business dealings (Amos 8:5; Neh 10:31; 13:15-18), and carrying burdens of any sort (Jer 17:21-22).

Accused of casuistry regarding what may or may not be done on the Sabbath, the rabbis actually relaxed certain Sabbath practices that were found in Intertestamental works such as the Book of Jubilees and the Zadokite Fragment.[13] The rabbis were concerned with the question, "What is meant by 'work'?" They deduced thirty-nine classes of work that would be prohibited on the Sabbath:

> sowing, ploughing, reaping, binding sheaves, threshing, winnowing, cleansing crops, grinding, sifting, kneading, baking, shearing wool, washing or beating or dyeing it, spinning, weaving, making two loops, weaving two threads, separating two threads, tying, loosening, sewing two stitches, tearing in order to sew two stitches, hunting a gazelle, slaughtering or flaying or salting it or curing its skin, scraping it or cutting it up, writing two letters, erasing in order to write two letters, building, pulling down, putting out a fire, lighting a fire, striking with a hammer and taking out anything from one domain into another. (*m. Šabb.* 7:2)

This list became even longer as these classes were minutely subdivided to cover more activities which were questioned as "work."

The rabbis also recognized that certain situations took priority even over the Sabbath. These cases were normally associated with cultic duties, defensive warfare, and the saving of life. A case regarding cultic duties was circumcision

[13]Cf. *Jub.* 50:8-12; Zadokite Document 10-11.

which usually occurred eight days after birth. If the date of circumcision fell on the Sabbath, the prohibitions regarding Sabbath were waived (cf. *m. Šabb.* 18:3; 19:1). Moreover, priestly work done in connection with the temple service such as baking cakes for the cereal offering was permissible on the Sabbath (*m. Tem.* 2:1).

One could also engage in military warfare to defend one's self on the Sabbath, a belief that went back to the time of the Maccabees. Upon hearing the report of a group of Jews who refused to fight on the Sabbath, Mattathias resolved that the Jews would defend themselves even if attacked on the Sabbath (1 Macc 2:29-41). The saving of life was the third case which superseded Sabbath regulations. Activities normally prohibited on the Sabbath could be done in cases of life or death emergencies. In an argument *a minori ad maius* (from the lesser to the greater), Rabbi Eleazar states: "If circumcision, which concerns one of a man's 248 members, overrides the Sabbath, how much more must his whole body (in danger of death) override the Sabbath (*b. Yoma* 85b; cf. *Mek. Šabbata* 1)."

Another aspect of Rabbinic theology regarding the Sabbath will be pertinent for our discussion of John's Gospel, viz., God's own activity on the seventh day. The rabbis were disturbed by the anthropomorphism that God "rested" on the seventh day. They came to believe that God remained active on the Sabbath for the physical governance of the universe (cf. Ps 121:4). Tinneus Rufus, the Roman governor who martyred Rabbi Akiba, once said to Akiba, "'If it is as you say that the Holy One, blessed be He, honors the Sabbath, then He should not stir up winds or cause the rain to fall on that day.' 'Woe to that man!' Akiba exclaimed: 'It is like one who carries objects four cubits'" *(Gen. Rab.* 11:5). According to the rule of *erub* a person was permitted to carry most objects in one's private domain or four cubits in the public domain. Akiba's point was that the whole universe is God's private and public domain. Therefore, when God moves the winds and the rains, it is to him like carrying something in one private ground which is permitted on the

Sabbath. Another explanation for God's activity was that just like work was permitted on the Sabbath in the Jerusalem temple, God remains active on the Sabbath since the universe is God's temple: "To you it shall be a holy day. To God however it is like a profane day (*Mek. Šabbata* 2)."

God's activity on the Sabbath not only covered the physical administration of the world but also its moral governance. Rabbi Phinehas quotes Rabbi Oshaya as saying: "When you say that God rested on this day from all his works, it means that he rested from the work of (creating) his world; but he did not rest from the work of the unrighteous and of the righteous" (*Gen. Rab.* 11:10). Furthermore, it was acknowledged that human beings were born and died on the Sabbath. Since only God can grant life and administer the fate of the person who died in judgment, God was active on the Sabbath in these two ways: in giving life and in judging over life at death (cf. *b. Ta'an.* 2a).

We are now in a position to summarize our findings on the Sabbath. Our discussion reveals that behind the Sabbath observance was a belief in the Creator-Redeemer God who gives to the Jewish people a holy day of rest. Not only a time for their own mental and spiritual re-creation, it was also a weekly time when they encountered God in worship. Thus God provided a model for them by resting on the seventh day after creating the world, although we saw how the rabbis modified this thought. Sabbath was a sign of God's perpetual covenant with the Jews, a day when they remembered the mighty things he has done on their behalf. Even amid their many prohibitions the rabbis never lost sight of the special covenantal significance of the Sabbath for the Jewish people. According to rabbinic *haggadah* which describes this significance in terms of a marriage,

> R. Simeon b. Yohai taught: The Sabbath pleaded to the Holy One, blessed be he: "All have a partner, while I have no partner!" "The community of Israel is your partner," God answered. And when Israel stood on Mount Sinai, God said to them: "Remember what I said to the Sabbath,

that the community of Israel is your partner, as it is said: 'Remember the Sabbath day to hallow it'" (Ex 20:8). (*Ex. Rab.* 11:8)

b. Sabbath in John 5:1-47

John begins Jesus' controversy with "the Jews" over the Sabbath in the Book of Signs in Jn 5:1-47, continues it in Jn 7:14-24, and culminates and concludes it in Jn 9:1-41. According to Jn 5:1 Jesus goes up to Jerusalem during "a feast of the Jews." The three annual pilgrimage feasts to Jerusalem consisted of Passover, Weeks (Pentecost), and Tabernacles. Hence, scholars have variously suggested that the feast was one of these three or one of two others that were not pilgrimage feasts: Rosh Hashanah (New Year) and Purim. We are not quite certain which feast the evangelist intended. We do know, however, that it was the Sabbath of that particular feast.

On that day Jesus encounters a man at the pool at Bethzatha (Bethesda) and cures him of his thirty-eight year illness. With the same command that Mk 2:9 attributes to Jesus, Jesus orders him: "Rise, take up your pallet, and walk" (Jn 5:8). In obeying Jesus, however, the healed man performs the last of the thirty-nine classes of work prohibited on the Sabbath, viz., carrying something from one domain to another. At first, the man is not able to identify Jesus to "the Jews" who point out his Sabbath transgression.[14] However, when Jesus finds the man in the temple and exhorts him to sin no more, the man in turn tells "the Jews" that it was Jesus who healed him. Jesus defends his actions before "the Jews" by maintaining, "My Father is working still, and I am working" (Jn 5:17). This, however, provokes "the Jews" even further because Jesus "not only broke the Sabbath but also called God his Father, making himself equal with God" (Jn 5:18).

[14]In this case the term "the Jews" refers here to the authorities, not the Jewish people since the healed man himself is a Jew.

Some commentators argue that the original story of the healing did not contain any mention of the Sabbath or the conflict that resulted from it. Instead, the evangelist obtained his core story, Jn 5:1-9ab, 14, from a tradition that was similar to the healing of the paralytic story in Mk 2:1-11. We already saw that Jn 5:8 was the same charge that Jesus gave to the paralytic in Mk 2:9. Mk 2:1-11 presupposed the belief that sickness or misfortune were God's punishment for sin. The fact that Jesus could heal thus demonstrated his ability to forgive sins. This message would also be the point of the original story in Jn 5:1-9ab, 14, a healing that concluded with Jesus' injunction, "See, you are well! Sin no more, that nothing worse befall you."

If these scholars are correct, the evangelist's transformation of the original tradition into a Sabbath controversy during a festival period would thus be very theologically significant. The conflict is focused on Jesus' explanation for his Sabbath healing in v 17, "My Father is working still, and I am working." Moreover, Jesus' discourse that follows in v 19-47 expands on v 17 as its defense. Let us discuss first Jn 5:17 and then the ensuing discourse.

We have already pointed out that rabbinic belief understood that God continues his creative and sustaining work even on the Sabbath. This rabbinic belief can be traced back to the Hebrew Bible itself where the Sabbath is linked both to Creation (Gen 2:2-3; Ex 20:8-11) and Redemption (Dt 5:15). The Creator-Redeemer God carries on his creative/liberating work throughout the course of salvation history. In view of this theology of the Sabbath, Jesus justifies the legality of his Sabbath healing by stating that he is doing the same redemptive work as his Father. The high Christology of Jesus' claim reflects the situation of the Johannine community in the post-70 era. It is this Christology that estranges the Johannine community from the Jewish community. For these Jews Jesus' defense condemns him on two counts: "because he not only broke the sabbath (an offense punishable by death) but also called God his Father, making himself equal with God (blasphemy)" (Jn 5:18).

By transforming the tradition into a Sabbath controversy, John is able, on one hand, to articulate Jesus' mysterious relationship to the Father, a theological affirmation that was bound to alienate the Jewish community. On the other hand, John is able to develop two related christological themes through this Sabbath dispute: Jesus as the one who gives life and Jesus as the one who judges.

The evangelist advances these two points in the discourse that results from this controversy, Jn 5:19-47. In reaction to the accusation that Jesus arrogates for himself equality with God, Jesus insists on his utter dependence on the Father throughout the discourse. Jesus can only do what the Father does. Two of these divine activities are giving life and judging:

> For as the Father raises the dead and gives them life, so also the Son gives life to whom he will. The Father judges no one, but has given all judgment to the Son, that all may honor the Son, even as they honor the Father. (Jn 5:21-23)

We have observed already that the giving and judging of life were activities acceptable for God to engage in on the Sabbath. They attested to God's continual saving work on the people's behalf. For John, God now acts through the Son, giving life and judging. Jesus' Sabbath command to the sick man in v 8, "Rise (*egeirein*), take up your pallet and walk," becomes more pregnant with meaning in v 21. Jesus' healing manifests his wider authority as God's son to grant life. As the Father raises (*egeirein*) the dead and gives them life (*zōopoiein*), so is the son empowered also.

The Sabbath healing is the third sign in the Book of Signs.[15] Its significance as a "sign" lies not merely in the healing alone, which itself is a dramatic event. Rather, the fact that it is a *Sabbath* healing empowers the event as a

[15]The first sign, Jn 2:1-11, is the changing of water into wine at the marriage feast at Cana. The second sign is in Jn 4:46-54 which just precedes the account of the Sabbath healing. It describes the healing of the official's son.

"sign." As Jesus' discourse makes clear, Jesus' healing work on the Sabbath reveals that he carries on the same life-giving/ life-judging activity of his Father. As God's son Jesus must work on the Sabbath.

c. The Sabbath in John 7:14-24

The controversy regarding the Sabbath described in John 5 is continued in Jn 7:14-24. The setting is the middle of the feast of Tabernacles and maybe even the Sabbath of that feast. If so, the conflict situation in 7:14-24 parallels that of 5:1-47 where the dispute takes place during the Sabbath of an unnamed feast. In fact, several commentators argue that 7:15-45 was displaced after John 6, but had originally formed the conclusion to the Sabbath controversy in John 5. They find several points of contact between John 5 and 7:15-24: 1) the objection in 7:15 correlates with 5:47; 2) Jesus' emphasis on his dependence on the one who sent him (5:19-23; 7:16-17); 3) the references to Moses (5:45-46; 7:19-23); 4) the reference "one work" (*en ergon*) in 7:21 refers back to the subject matter of John 5 and forms a catchword with 5:20, 36; and 5) the references to one's own glory and God's glory (5:41, 44; 7:18).

The conflict in Jn 7:14-24 occurs when Jesus is teaching in the temple for the first time during the feast of Tabernacles. The detail in v 14 that Jesus is in the temple teaching is significant. We have already noted that priestly duties in the temple were exempt from the Sabbath law. Furthermore, Jesus uses an example from cultic ceremonies that took precedence over the Sabbath, viz., circumcision, in his own argument for the Sabbath healing. John seems to be incorporating these details not only to underscore the legality of Jesus' ministry even according to Jewish law, but also to intimate more who this person Jesus is. We compare John with Mt 12:5-6:

> Have you not read in the law how on the Sabbath the priests in the temple profane the Sabbath, and are guilt-

> less? *I tell you, something greater than the temple is here.* (Mt 12:5-6)

"The Jews" marvel at Jesus' teaching because Jesus never formally studied Scripture and its interpretation under the sponsorship of a recognized rabbi. In reply, Jesus grounds his teaching authority not in an earthly source but in a divine one: in the God who sent him into the world. Moving onto the offensive, Jesus then accuses "the Jews" of not keeping the law of Moses. This accusation contrasts with the evangelist's portrayal of Jesus in accord with the correct interpretation of the law. In his question, "Why do you seek to kill me?" (v 19), Jesus is most likely referring to the plot of the Jewish authorities to kill him because of his alleged Sabbath violation and blasphemy (cf. Jn 5:18 and 7:1).

Jesus presents another argument for his Sabbath work which, in contrast to those advanced in John 5, would cohere with rabbinic teaching at the time. Cognizant that circumcision is an activity that takes precedence over the Sabbath, Jesus argues *a minori ad maius* (from the lesser to the greater) that the healing of a person's whole body would also demand a waiver of the Sabbath prohibition. Jesus' logic is similar to the argument of Rabbi Eleazar which we cited on p. 37 above (cf. *t. Šabb.* 15:16). He exhorts his audience not to judge by appearances, but with right judgment. His accusers saw only the pallet carried on the Sabbath and not the healing of the infirmed person. They ignored another important aspect of the Sabbath, viz., acknowledging God's continual redemptive activity in one's humanitarian response toward the underprivileged sectors of society. Sabbath was created for the expressed purpose of "remembering" or "re-presenting" the mighty acts God has done for the people. In their adherence to the letter of the Sabbath law, "the Jews" forgot the redemptive purpose for which the law was given.

d. Sabbath in John 9:1-41

The story of the healing of the blind man in John 9 is the

sixth sign of the Book of Signs. It is here that John develops his Sabbath Christology most fully. The occasion of this second Sabbath healing results in a Pharisaic court proceeding, where the opinions regarding the "offence" are divided. It will be significant that the resourceful defendant is not Jesus but the healed man, whom the Pharisees accuse of being "his disciple" (9:28). We will see that John 9 most probably reflects the circumstances of the evangelist's time rather than Jesus' time. The healed blind man represents those of the Johannine community who felt a strong animosity from the Jewish community for their belief in Jesus. Intimations of John's Sabbath Christology are introduced at the onset. In response to his disciples' query whether or not the man's blindness was due to his own sins or that of his parents, Jesus replies that it was the result of neither. Rather, the man is blind, in order that

> the *works* of God might be made manifest in him. We must *work* the *works* of him who sent me, while it is day; night comes, when no one can *work*. (Jn 9:3-4)

The repeated catchword, "work" (*ergon*), recalls 5:17 and 7:21 where Jesus maintains that, as his Father who sent him into the world does not interrupt his creative and redemptive enterprise, so too does Jesus not stop his own saving work on the Sabbath. By the use of the catchword, John foreshadows here the Sabbath controversy to come. We point out that the evangelist does not yet relate the detail that it is the Sabbath. As in the case of John 5, he presents this piece of information only after the healing takes place.

Jesus heals the blind man by making a mud pack from his spittle and dirt, smearing it on the man's eyes, and enjoining him to wash in the pool of Siloam (v 6-7. Cf. Mk 8:23). The healed man is then brought to the Pharisees, at which point the evangelist informs the reader that "it was a sabbath day when Jesus made the clay and opened (the man's) eyes" (v 13). In contrast to John 5, Jesus, not the healed person, is culpable of transgressing the Sabbath. It would appear to these Pharisees that Jesus violates two Sabbath prohibitions. Among the thirty-nine classes of work forbidden on the Sabbath is "kneading" and Jesus "kneads" the spittle and dirt to make the mud pack. Moreover, Jesus heals *on the Sabbath* a person whose life is not in any immediate danger. From the Pharisees' point of view, Jesus could have postponed this activity for the following day.

Differing interpretations of Jesus' act create a division in the Pharisaic assembly:

> Some of the Pharisees said, "This man is not from God, for he does not keep the sabbath." But others said, "How can a man who is a sinner do such signs?" (Jn 9:16)

As these opinions reveal, Jesus' "sign" can be considered from two different vantage points. One can view the "sign" as "work" performed on the Sabbath and, hence, a transgression of the law. Or, one can regard the "sign" as a miraculous "work" of God that transcends the law. From the first point of view, Jesus is a "sinner"; from the second, Jesus is "from God." John will equate the first position with "blindness," the second with "discipleship."

The Pharisees take an alternative course to deal with the division in their ranks: they try to deny that the man had ever been blind, thus repudiating the healing and, at the same time, that Jesus is "from God." They enlist the testimony of the healed man's parents to confirm his congenital blindness and explain the fact of his sight (v 18). The parents verify their son's lifelong blindness but refuse to commit themselves further to an explanation of his present sight. The reason given is that "they feared the Jews, for the Jews had already agreed that if any one should confess him to be Christ, he was to be put out of the synagogue" (v 22). The post-70 conflict between the Johannine community and the synagogue is here reflected back into the ministry of Jesus.

The Pharisees return to the healed man and try to bully him into admitting that Jesus is a sinner. They become more blind just as the once blind man acquires more penetrating insights into the person of Jesus.[16] To thwart the Pharisees the man resorts to rabbinic logic based on two undeniable facts: that he who was once blind can now see and that God does not listen to sinners. He concludes reasonably that "If this man were not from God, he could do nothing." And like the true disciple of John's own community, the healed man is expelled from the Jewish community (vv 24-34).

e. Summary

The Fourth Evangelist uses his thoroughly Jewish understanding of the Sabbath as a vehicle to articulate his high Christology. Face to face with the theology of Sabbath and the laws regarding "keeping" it is the person of Jesus. From John's christological perspective, Jesus in no way violates the Sabbath when he heals the ailing. Like his Father, he cannot rest on the Sabbath from the creative and liberative work governing the world. He must carry on the life-giving and life-judging commission for which he was sent into this world by the Father.

The "signs" that Jesus performs on the Sabbath have two levels of meaning. To those who deny that Jesus is "from God," who are "blind" to the "works" accomplished in the name of his Father, Jesus' signs are transgressions of the Sabbath law and a manifestation of his sinfulness. This is the picture which the evangelist paints of the post-70 Jews who found the Christology of the Johannine community sacrilegious. On the other hand, for those who come to believe in Jesus as God's very son, these signs demonstrate the truth of his words. Because of their Christology they are severed from the synagogue and the Jewish people. However, their faith in Jesus replaces what they lost. Their response to this person is epitomized in the confession of the healed blind

[16]The healed man first acknowledges that the man who healed him was "called Jesus" (v 11). He then declares that he is a "prophet" (v 17), and that he is "from God" (v 33). Finally, he confesses to Jesus that he "believes in the Son of Man" (vv 35-39).

man at the conclusion of the story: "'Lord, I believe'; and he worshipped him" (9:37).

2

Passover

a. Passover in the Hebrew Bible

The feast of Passover was one of the principal festivals of the Jewish liturgical year and has remained so even to this day. On one level, it commemorates the passage of winter to spring, when the whole earth is reborn and comes to life again. On another level, it celebrates the dramatic liberation of the Jewish people by their all-powerful God from their slavery in Egypt. And still on another level, it affirms the liberation of all men and women from every form of enslavement and oppression, envisioning life amid the appearance and realities of death.

For the Jewish people, Passover does not simply celebrate ritually a "freedom from" but also a "freedom to": a freedom to worship their God in the wilderness and become God's own people. The feast brings to consciousness the story of their hasty preparations for the journey, their flight from the powerful Egyptian charioteers who were intent on reenslaving them, their dashed hopes and despair when confronted with the body of water that separated them from freedom. Moreover, it is the story of their God who triumphed over their oppressors at the Sea of Reeds, who fed them with manna and quails in the wilderness, who gave them drink from the rock, who led them ultimately to the holy mountain of Sinai to ratify a covenant with them.

One finds the story about the Exodus and its ritualization

in the feast of Passover in the Book of Exodus, chapters 11-15. The structure of these chapters by the Priestly editor is quite revealing of his theological intent. A reader is usually struck by the long sections of liturgical instructions that seemingly interrupt the actual story of the Exodus from Egypt. We display the literary design of these chapters in the following:

Literary Structure of Exodus 11—15

A. God's Foretelling of the Tenth Plague: The Death of the Egyptian Firstborn (Exodus 11)

Injunctions Regarding the Passover celebration (Ex 12:1-28)

B. Resumption of Plague Narrative: The Actual Death of the Egyptian Firstborn (Ex 12:29-51)

Injunctions Regarding Ritual Consecration of The Firstborn (Ex 13:1-16)

C. Narrative Account of the Deliverance at the Sea of Reeds (Ex 13:17-14:31)

Liturgical Rehearsal of the Deliverance at the Sea of Reeds—the Song of Moses (Ex 15:1-18)

Notice that the Priestly editor "sandwiches" the blocks of liturgical material between the narrative accounts of the story. The literary effect of this structure keeps in tension the historical event that happened "long ago" and the liturgical rehearsal of that event "here and now" in the Passover celebration. Like the festal day of Sabbath, the feast of Passover is to be a "day of remembrance" for every generation of the Jewish people (Ex 12:14). During this feast the community "makes present" liturgically the central story of its liberation from Egypt.

The liturgical sections of Exodus 11-13 disclose three different ceremonies of the Passover feast: the Passover sacrifice, the feast of Unleavened Bread, and the consecration of the firstborn. These practices were originally separate from each other. In all probability, they were not Israelite in origin, but rather were customs that the Israelites adopted from their ancient near eastern neighbors. These secular feasts had their own particular meaning before they were later associated with the historical event of the Exodus. It is the original purposes of these feasts that we now explore in order to determine their theological reinterpretation by the Israelites.

The Passover sacrifice was initially a nomadic rite observed by shepherds at the spring of the year, the time when they would migrate to the highlands to pasture their flock. The sacrifice of a young animal was offered to insure the fertility and safety of the flock as it made the journey to greener pastures. The blood shed in the sacrifice was sprinkled on the tent poles to protect the inhabitants from malevolent spirits. All of the aspects of the ritual underscored the nomadic lifestyle of those who partook in it. The animal was roasted whole over a fire. It was eaten with bitter herbs that were picked wild in the desert. Those who participated in the ritual ate as though they were readied for a journey with sandals on their feet and with staff in hand. The ancient Israelite tribes most likely observed this nomadic ritual long before they settled in Egypt and later adapted this ritual when they settled in the agrarian society of Canaan.

While the Passover sacrifice had its beginnings in a nomadic society, the feast of Unleavened Bread (*maṣṣôt*) had its home in an agricultural society. The Israelites adopted and adapted this feast when they made the transition from a nomadic to an agricultural style of life after the conquest of Canaan. The first of three feasts held during the agricultural year, the feast of Unleavened Bread marked the beginning of the barley harvest near time of the spring solstice in March or April. During the feast, the people discarded all leavened bread and old leaven of the past year. For the first seven days of the barley harvest, they partook only of unleavened bread made from the newly gathered grain, an action symbolizing a new beginning. Fifty days afterwards came the

Feasts of Weeks (*Shavuot* or Pentecost) which heralded the conclusion of the grain season in the harvesting of wheat. Finally, in autumn the feast of Booths celebrated the harvesting of grapes, olives, and fruits that ripened over the long hot summer period.

Like the feast of Passover, the consecration of the firstborn probably originated among a nomadic people. The firstborn was a sign of a new couple's fertility and was thought to embody their best qualities. Since the new life would not be possible without the favor of the Deity, the firstborn sons of human beings were dedicated to God, while the firstborn of animals were offered to God in sacrifice.

Eventually, these three separate feasts were joined into one Israelite celebration called Passover (*pēsaḥ*). However, it is not exactly certain when they were joined and when they became associated with the Exodus event. At some point in time they were translated from their nomadic or agricultural contexts and became one "historicized" feast, a feast commemorating a saving act of God in the history of the Israelite people.

Aspects of each feast were reinterpreted in light of the Exodus event. The consideration for safety on a journey that marked the nomadic feast of Passover now became a concern of the Israelites as they embarked from Egypt. The features of a nomadic lifestyle, e.g., the roasting of the animal whole, eating the meal as if beginning a journey, now represented a people in flight from their oppressive taskmasters. The unleavened bread symbolized the haste of the people who had no time to allow their bread to rise. Moreover, it continued to represent the new beginning for the people as they took their first steps on their road to freedom. The consecration of the firstborn was now connected with the immolation of the paschal lamb. The blood of the lamb sprinkled on the doorpost now marked the people as firstborn sons and daughters of God, while the firstborn sons of the Egyptians were slaughtered.

Exodus 12 contained two traditions regarding the instructions on celebrating Passover. Scholars usually attributed

Ex 12:1-20 to the Priestly (P) writer during the Exile and Ex 12:21-27 to the Yahwist's (J) pen during the time of the United Monarchy. In the earlier Yahwist tradition Moses assembled the elders and charged them to select lambs for their families and kill them for the passover. With sprigs of hyssop, a bush used in various rites of purification (cf. Num 19:6), they would anoint their doorpost and lintels with the blood of the lamb. Accordingly, the "destroyer" would not be allowed to strike the inhabitants of a house that had blood on it. Parents educating their children regarding the meaning of the Passover celebration would say to them:

> It is the sacrifice of the Lord's passover, for he passed over the houses of the people of Israel in Egypt, when he slew the Egyptians but spared our houses. (Ex 12:27)

The blood did not merely serve to shield the Israelites from the effects of the destroyer, as the blood in the original nomadic rite protected one from the evil spirits. Instead, it had a positive significance arising from the associations that blood had with life itself (cf. Dt 12:23; Lev 17:11). It served to mark the Israelites as firstborn sons and daughters who were to remain alive. The Exodus event was a question of sonship. God had instructed Moses to say to Pharaoh:

> Thus says the Lord, "Israel is my firstborn son, and I say to you, 'Let my son go that he may serve me; if you refuse to let him go, behold I will slay your firstborn son.'" (Ex 4:22-23)

As the story goes, Pharaoh refused to release the Israelites to worship their God. The tenth plague consequently had symbolic meaning. The destroyer took Pharaoh's own firstborn son and those of his people in return for the sonship and daughtership of the people of Israel. The paschal blood purified and marked the Jews as God's children. They were now made holy to offer worship to their God in the wilderness.

The Priestly version of the instructions for Passover developed further aspects of the ritual. In 12:1 God fixed the time of Passover in the liturgical calendar for Moses and Aaron. Unlike Ex 23:15 and 34:18 which designated the old Canaanite month of Abib as the month to celebrate the Passover, Ex 12:2 simply stated: "This month shall be for you the beginning of months; it shall be the first month of the year for you." During the postexilic period this month came to be known by its Babylonian name, Nisan. On the 14th of Nisan, the feast of Passover was observed. On the next day, the 15th of Nisan, the feast of Unleavened Bread began and lasted seven days (cf. Lev 23:5-8; Num 28:16-25).

In contrast to the J account, the Priestly writer was very exact regarding liturgical dates and specifications. On the 10th of Nisan every household selected a lamb, a year old male without blemish taken from either the sheep or the goats. The lamb was then slaughtered on the evening of the 14th of Nisan. As in the J account, the blood of the sacrifice was put on the doorpost and lintels. However, unlike the J story the P version contained a careful description of the Passover meal, not a relaxed meal, but one eaten in haste by people ready to move (vv 7-10). The reason given for such a meal highlighted the idea of Israel as the firstborn children of God:

> It is the Lord's passover. For I will pass through the land of Egypt that night, and I will smite all the firstborn in the land of Egypt, both human and beast; and on all the gods of Egypt I will execute judgments: I am the Lord. The blood shall be a *sign* for you, upon the houses where you are; and when I see the blood, I will pass over you, and no plague shall fall upon you to destroy you, when I smite the land of Egypt. (Ex 12:11-13)

The blood became a sign of life before God. We have already seen the Priestly writer's theology of signs in our discussion of the Sabbath. The Sabbath became a sign of God's covenant with the people. Similarly, the blood of the Passover sacrifice—the token of life—symbolized Israel's new position as God's own children. Like the Sabbath, Passover became a "day of remembrance," a feast dedicated to God observed by every generation thereafter (12:14). In the celebration the Jews "relived" for themselves their ancestors' experience of slavery and liberation of long ago. Every aspect of the feast assisted in recreating this momentous event of old.

The communal element of the Passover meal was noteworthy. All Israelites were to eat this meal at the same time, in groups big enough to consume the whole lamb (12:3-4). Anyone who was not circumcised was not permitted to join in this meal (12:43). These details underscored the fact that God did not merely save individual Israelites; God liberated a people. The true Israelite was one who identified him or herself as a member of a people—a people who had been in bondage and had been delivered from it. This person was one who incorporated the people's experience into his or her own existential situation. This person was one who, aware of his or her own condition as slave and desiring freedom, was willing to follow God into the wilderness and there worship God with the rest of Israel. Sharing in the Passover at the same time, each group was conscious of the fact that it was united with all of Israel at that moment. In the development of Hebrew cult, the lamb could only be sacrificed at the temple in Jerusalem. This unity of sacrifice further served to remind the individual group that it was a member of a larger unit, the people.

The Hebrew Bible associated the celebration of the Passover with pivotal events in the history of the Jewish people. The next mention of the feast after the Exodus event was Joshua's Passover after he led the people across the Jordan into the Promised Land (Josh 5:10-12). Hundreds of years later Josiah, king of Judah (640-609 B.C.E.), culminated his massive religious reform program with the celebration of the Passover (2 Kings 23:21-23 = 2 Chron 35:1-18). The destruction of the first temple in Jerusalem by the Babylonians under Nebuchadnezzar and the exile of the religious and political leadership of the Jews in 587 B.C.E. disrupted the customary celebration of Passover which had been localized at the temple. Nevertheless, the exilic prophet Ezekiel envisioned a future time when the temple would be rebuilt and the Passover observed again (Ezek 45:21-24). Ezekiel's vision was realized when Cyrus of Persia defeated the Babylonians and allowed the Jews to return to their homeland in 538 B.C.E. with the sacred vessels that Nebuchadnezzar carried away from the temple (Ezra 1:2-11). In spite of much resistance by the Samaritans, the temple was rebuilt and dedicated. The first feast which the returning exiles observed in the newly constructed "house of God" was the feast of Passover (Ezra 6:19-22).

Of these particular events cited in the Hebrew Bible when Passover was celebrated, we focus on the first: the first Passover in Canaan under Moses' successor, Joshua. This particular Passover will have relevance for our discussion of the Fourth Gospel. It is very likely that Joshua 5 was a Passover *haptarah*, i.e., a reading from the Prophets for the synagogue service, during the time of Jesus (cf. *b. Meg.* 31a). Joshua has just led the people across the Jordan into the promised land to the ancient sanctuary of Gilgal. At Gilgal he has the people circumcised since no one who was uncircumcised could join in the Passover (Ex 12:48). The account of the feast is as follows:

> While the people of Israel were encamped in Gilgal they kept the passover on the fourteenth day of the month at evening in the plains of Jericho. And on the morrow after the passover, on that very day, they ate of the produce of the land, unleavened cakes and parched grain. And the manna ceased on the morrow, when they ate of the produce of the land; and the people of Israel had manna no more, but ate of the fruit of the land of Canaan that year. (Josh 5:10-12)

We note the connection between the feast of Passover and the feast of Unleavened Bread which was celebrated on the following day. Significant is the detail that the manna which had nourished the Israelites in the wilderness stopped falling when they began to enjoy the produce of Canaan. Called the "bread from heaven" (Ex 16:4; cf. Neh 9:15), manna was here associated with the feast of Passover. Later Jewish tradition would develop this association. According to *Mek. Vayassa'* 2:18-25, manna fell for the first time on the 15th of the second month, Iyyar, the date associated with the Passover by those who missed its celebration during the month of Nisan (Num 9:11). *Gen. Rab.* 48:12 related that the bread which Abraham and Sarah baked for the three men (Gen 18:6) was baked at the time of Passover and it anticipated the manna given to Israel in the Wilderness of Sin.

Besides its association with Passover and the events surrounding the Exodus, manna was also connected with God's "word" or commandment which gave life. One reads in Dt 8:2-3:

> You shall remember all the way which the Lord your God had led you these forty years in the wilderness, that he might humble you, testing you to know what was in your heart, whether you would keep his commandments or not. And he humbled you and let you hunger and fed you with manna, which you did not know, nor did your ancestors know; that he might make you know that one does not live by bread alone, but one lives by everything that proceeds out of the mouth of the Lord.

According to Wis 16:20-21, manna was the "food of angels," the "bread from heaven" that suited the taste of each Israelite. As in Dt 8:2-3, Wis 16:26 stated that manna, not just material nourishment, was a symbol for God's "word" which granted life to those who trusted in God. Although the manna given by Moses was not explicitly identified as the Torah (law) given by Moses, these texts made strong connections between the two. The connections were clearer in Neh 9:13-15 where the gifts of the "bread from heaven" and the water from the rock were mentioned immediately after the giving of the Torah by Moses. These themes were resumed again in Neh 9:20: "You gave your good Spirit to instruct them, and did not withhold your manna from their mouth and gave them water to drink." The rabbinic tradition would identify "bread" with the Torah that Lady Wisdom offered the people when she enjoined them in Prov 9:5, "Come, eat of my bread" (*Gen. Rab. 70:5).*

Manna took on messianic connotations in later Jewish thought. The manna that stopped falling when the Israelites entered the Promised Land would fall again in the messianic age. According to *2 Apoc. Bar.* 29:8, "the treasury of manna will come down again from on high, and they will eat of it in those years, because these are they who have arrived at the consummation of time." Commenting on Eccl 1:9, "there is nothing new under the sun," Rabbi Isaac (ca. 300) was quoted as saying that the latter Redeemer would cause the manna to fall just as the former Redeemer, Moses, caused the manna to descend (*Eccl. Rab.* I, 9, 1). About manna *Mek. Vayassa'* 5, 63-65 stated, "You will not find it in this world, but you will find it in the world to come." We will return to these manna themes in our discussion of John 6.

b. Passover During the Time of Jesus

We saw in the preceding section that the feast of Passover commemorated the fundamental event of the Jewish people, their liberation from Egypt. Through the event they were marked as God's children by the blood of the lamb and made ready to worship God in the wilderness. A complex of symbols and themes were "remembered" in the feast: the lamb, the unleavened bread and bitter herbs all hastily prepared for a communal meal; the blood on the doorpost; the deliverance through the walls of water; the manna that provided sustenance and the water that quenched the people's thirst in the wilderness; all of God's mighty acts on the people's behalf, culminating in the ratification of the covenant and the giving of the law on Mount Sinai. By the time of Jesus, it was highly likely that the Passover feast and its rich symbolism took on messianic overtones.

With the construction of the first temple in Jerusalem by

Solomon, the nature of the Passover feast was transformed. During the Golden Age of the United Monarchy, the city of Jerusalem not only bound the tribes politically together by becoming their national center, but also united them religiously as their cultic center. In Jerusalem the temple and the most sacred ark of the covenant was situated. With the centralization of the cult, Passover moved from being a domestic observance to one of the three national pilgrimage feasts along with the feasts of Weeks and Tabernacles. Although the festal pilgrimages were disrupted with the destruction of Solomon's temple by the Babylonians, they were resumed with the construction of the second temple after the exile.

Hence, during the first century when Jesus lived, Passover was a national pilgrimage festival focused in the sanctuary in Jerusalem. About 100,000 pilgrims joined the 50,000 residents of Jerusalem during the Passover season, occupying every available space within the walled city and the surrounding area. It was in the excitement and confusion of one such pilgrimage that the young boy, Jesus, stayed behind in Jerusalem without his parents' knowledge (Lk 2:41-44).

In the afternoon on the day before Passover, all of the Passover animals were ritually slaughtered and offered up to God in the temple.[17] This sacrifice was prepared and eaten during a meal in the temple precincts or, because of the large number of crowds, in the city of Jerusalem itself. As in the earlier domestic Passover, the eating of the sacrificed animal in prescribed groups was the central feature of the Passover meal. Moreover, the unleavened bread and the bitter herbs were consumed along with the animal as in earlier times. The ceremony for the Passover meal consisted of three main divisions: the sacrificial meal itself; the *haggadah*, i.e., the recounting of the story of the Exodus and its meaning for the Passover participants; and lastly, the songs of praise to God which were usually drawn from the Psalms.

[17]Although Ex 12:6 commanded that the lambs be killed on the evening of the 14th of Nisan, the ritual slaughter began earlier when the lamb had to be sacrificed in the temple to accommodate the large numbers of animals.

The Passover meal during Jesus' time was not the ritualized meal called the *seder* which is celebrated by the Jews of today. *Seder* means "order" in Hebrew and it refers to the ritual order of service for the Passover meal. The *seder* came into being after 70 C.E. as a response to the destruction of the second temple. The ruin of the temple meant the end of the ritual slaughtering of the Passover lambs, and hence, the loss of the main course of the sacrificial meal. Under the very subtle pastoral guidance of the early rabbis, the sacrificial Passover meal evolved slowly into the non-sacrificial *seder* during the post-70 period. The celebration was transferred from the temple to the domestic family setting, as in the earlier days of the feast. In the absence of the sacrificial lamb, the unleavened bread and bitter herbs were given a greater significance. A didactic emphasis on the symbolic interpretation of the three foods gradually replaced the literal act of eating the foods.

Particularly noteworthy was the rabbis' theological restructuring of the sacrificial meal to focus on a future redemption of the people. God did not simply redeem the people in the past Exodus event. Rather, God continued to save the people and would do so in the years to come. Envisioned was the reconstruction of another temple in Jerusalem. This hope for future redemption, which was not a feature of the pre-70 sacrificial meal, was expressed clearly at the conclusion of the *seder*: "This year here, next year in the land of Israel; this year as slaves, next year as free."[18]

c. Passover in the Gospel of John: Introduction

Unlike the Synoptic Gospels, John's gospel recounts three Passovers during Jesus' ministry, instead of just one at the end of his ministry in Jerusalem. The first Passover in the Fourth Gospel occurs at the beginning of Jesus' work in Jerusalem after he performs his first sign at Cana (Jn 2:13-

[18]For further information on the *seder*, consult Baruch M. Bokser, "Was the Last Supper a Passover Seder?" *Bible Review* 3 (1987) 24-33.

25). The second Passover in Galilee provides the backdrop for his discourse on the bread of life (John 6). Finally, the third Passover occurs at the end of Jesus' ministry in Jerusalem, where he shares his last meal with his disciples and is condemned and put to death (John 13-19). All three Passover accounts contain John's theme of the replacement of Jewish institutions and beliefs. In the first Passover, Jesus replaces the temple. In the second, Moses and the manna are replaced, and in the third, the Passover lambs sacrificed in the temple.

Besides these three Passovers, John's gospel is full of Exodus/ Passover imagery. At the outset of the gospel, John the Baptist witnesses to Jesus, saying, "Behold, the Lamb of God, who takes away the sin of the world" (2:29. cf. 2:36). The evangelist's symbol of the lamb incorporates Old Testament features of both the sacrificial Passover lamb and the lamb as the Suffering Servant who, bearing the sins of many, is led to slaughter (Isaiah 53). We will soon discover how the evangelist structures his Passion narrative so that Jesus' crucifixion coincides with the ritual slaughter of the Passover lambs in the temple. Moreover, John also draws several parallels between Moses, who figures so prominently in the Exodus/Passover narratives, and the person of Jesus (cf. 1:17; 5:45-47; 6:31). Jn 3:14 refers to an incident in the wilderness recounted in Num 21:8, where Moses raises a bronze serpent on a pole at God's command. All who were bitten by the venomous snakes and who gazed upon the serpent would be healed. In John, the Son of Man is the one who is lifted up so that whoever believes in him will have eternal life. We will observe further correspondences in the Passover texts to which we now turn.

d. The First Passover: Jn 2:13-25

In contrast to the Synoptics who place the account of the cleansing of the temple at the end of Jesus' ministry (Mk 11:15-17; Mt 21:12-13; Lk 19:45-46), John's gospel situates it at the beginning of the ministry *and* during the feast of Passover. Jesus had just performed his first sign, the changing of water to wine at the wedding feast at Cana (2:1-11). Jesus' miracle fits in well with John's theology of the replacement of Jewish institutions and feasts: Jesus replaces the water used in Jewish rites of purification (2:6) with the finest of wines. Moreover, the setting of a wedding feast and the abundance of wine recall the ancient promises of a messianic banquet where wine and food will be plentiful (Isa 55:1-3; Jer 31:12; Am 9:13-14. Cf. *1 Enoch* 10:19; *2 Apoc. Bar.* 29:5). For John, Jesus' sign is a manifestation that the messianic age is at hand.

After the miracle at Cana, Jesus goes on pilgrimage from Galilee up to Jerusalem for the Passover festivities. Prior to the actual feast itself, Jesus encounters merchants selling oxen, sheep, and pigeons, as well as money changers in the Court of the Gentiles of the temple precincts. The animal vendors and money changers catered to the many pilgrims who wished to buy animals for the Passover sacrifice in Jerusalem itself rather than bring them along on pilgrimage. Such business transactions were customary and economically necessary for the temple to function. Jesus, however, drives them out with a whip, accusing them of making "my Father's house a house of trade" (2:16). John's account of Jesus' accusation differs from the Synoptics' version where Jesus is angry because of the dishonesty occurring in the temple: "You have made (the house of prayer) a den of robbers" (cf. Mk 11:17).

Stringent criticism of the temple and its cultic abuses have a strong precedent in the prophets, especially Jeremiah whom the Synoptics quote in their rendition of the story (Jer 7:11. Cf. Hos 4:4-6; Mic 7:6-8). Furthermore, the reform of the cult is a feature of Jewish eschatological expectations. According to Mal 3:1-4, God's messenger will prepare the way for God's sudden coming into the temple by purifying its priesthood and cult. In another messianic passage that is significant for John's cleansing of the temple story, Zechariah concludes his prophecy by stating, "And there shall no longer be a trader in the house of the Lord of hosts on that day" (Zech 14:21).

While the criticism in the Synoptics' cleansing of the temple accounts argues for a genuine reform of the temple and its cult, John's gospel maintains that the trading itself is wrong. Moreover, since commercial transactions are necessary for the temple sacrifices during the Passover season, the critique of the Johannine Jesus implies a fundamental opposition to the temple itself. Indeed, responding to "the Jews" who demand a sign of his authority, Jesus states enigmatically, "Destroy this temple and in three days I will raise it up" (Jn 2:19). Jesus refers both to the actual temple, which would have been destroyed by the time of John's gospel, and to "the temple of his body" (2:21), which will die and rise after three days. John here anticipates Jesus' eventual death as the Passover Lamb of God during Jesus' third Passover at the end of his work on earth. For John, the person of Jesus supersedes and replaces the earthly temple. Since the Father dwells not in the Holy of Holies of the temple, but in the person of Jesus (Jn 14:10), Jesus becomes the new spiritual temple through whom the Father is worshipped (Jn 4:21-23).

Similarities as well as contrasts exist between the Cana miracle and the story of the cleansing of the temple at Passover that follows it. Both stories reveal who Jesus is during a particular festival, the former in Galilee, the latter in Jerusalem. In Cana, the wedding feast is a joyous celebration among Jesus' own people in northern Palestine. The Passover feast in Jerusalem, however, is marked by hostility and conflict with "the Jews." Both stories feature John's theology of the replacement of Jewish institutions and feasts. During the wedding feast Jesus replaces the water for the Jewish purification rites with the best of wine. During the feast of Passover, Jesus prophesies that his body will replace the holy temple in Jerusalem. Both stories communicate that, for John, the messianic age is at hand in the person of Jesus. The abundance of wine in a wedding context recalls the prophecies of the future messianic banquet where wine will flow without end. The cleansing of the temple evokes the messages of the prophets who foretell of a purification of temple and cult by God's "messenger." Moreover, the conclusions of both accounts are similar in structure, giving clues to the identity of Jesus and the proper response of those who encounter him:

> This, the first of his signs, Jesus did at Cana in Galilee, and manifested his glory; and his disciples believed in him. (Jn 2:11)
>
> Now when he was in Jerusalem at the Passover feast, many believed in his name when they saw the signs which he did; but Jesus did not trust himself to them, because he knew them all and needed no one to bear witness to human nature; for he himself knew what was in the human heart. (Jn 2:23-25)

According to 2:11, the signs reveal the "glory" of Jesus, but only to those who regard them with the eyes of faith. This "glory" is the Father's creative power given to Jesus which will be manifested fully at the "hour" of Jesus' death and resurrection (12:23; 17:24). The true response of his disciples in witnessing this revelation is faith (cf. also 20:30-31). They come to believe this person as the one sent by the Father, who called them to follow him, promising them, "You shall see greater things than these" (1:50).

The theme of belief is likewise found in 2:23-25, but with a qualification. Just prior to these concluding verses of the cleansing of the temple account, John relates that after the resurrection, the disciples recalled Jesus' remark about the temple of his body which will be raised in three days "and they believed the scriptures and the word which Jesus had spoken" (2:22). John contrasts their belief with the inadequate faith of those in Jerusalem. Many during this Passover season also came to believe, but only because they witnessed the miraculous signs that Jesus performed (cf. 4:48). They did not discern in the "sign" a revelation of who Jesus really was. The themes of true faith and inadequate faith, as well as messianic fulfillment and replacement, anticipate their development in Jesus' bread-of-life discourse set during his next Passover season in Galilee.

e. The Second Passover: John 6

The context of Jesus' fourth and fifth signs, viz., his multiplication of the loaves and his walking upon the water in Galilee, as well as his ensuing bread-of-life discourse, is the second Passover of his ministry. Although much has been written on this theologically rich chapter, we will only present how the evangelist capitalizes on his knowledge of the Jewish feast of Passover to advance his particular Christology.

First of all, the evangelist draws a striking contrast between Jesus and the person of Moses, who figures so prominently in the Exodus/Passover traditions. Moses, the powerful leader of the Jewish people who performed wondrous signs for them, who guided them from slavery to freedom through the walls of water, who fed them with manna in the desert and gave them drink, who saw God face to face on the mountain of Sinai and was their mediator in the giving of the Law; this Moses, for John, will be superseded and replaced by the person of Jesus.

The first hint of the Moses traditions is the detail that Jesus went up the mountain and sat down there with his disciples (6:3). Moses continually went up the mountain to encounter God on Sinai (Ex 19:3, 20; 24:12-13). Moreover, the evangelist's detail recalls Ex 24:9-11 where Moses and the elders go up the mountain and partake of the covenantal meal in God's presence. The miracle of the loaves soon to occur will symbolize a new covenant which will be ratified by Jesus. Jesus' question to Philip, "How are we to buy bread, so that these people may eat?" is similar to the question that Moses asks of God in Num 11:13, "Where am I to get meat to give all this people?"

The feeding of the people by Jesus at Passover time evokes images of the manna which Moses gave to the Israelites in the wilderness. This correlation is highly significant, for we saw in the above discussion of the manna traditions that God will not feed the people again until the messianic age. Moreover, the abundance of food baskets left over after the people were satiated (v 13) again recalls the messianic banquet. In the case of the miracle at Cana, the best of wine abounds; here, loaves aplenty.

Experiencing this sign, the crowd proclaims, "This is indeed the prophet who is to come into the world" (v 14)! This identification is most likely associated with Dt 18:15-22 where God will raise up a prophet like Moses from among the people. A messianic interpretation of Dt 18:15-22 was popular among the Samaritan and Qumran sects and was likely "in the air" among the common populace during Jesus' time. Given the time of Passover when the Messiah was thought to appear and Jesus' resemblance to their former powerful leader Moses, the people rush to make him their king (v 15). However, perceiving the people's misunderstanding of his sign, and thus who he really is, Jesus withdraws to the mountain by himself.

The next incident is the sign of the walking upon the water, where Jesus reveals himself to his disciples through the divine name, "I AM" (v 20). One observes Passover symbolism here in the reference to the crossing of the Sea of Reeds in the Exodus from Egypt. John perhaps recalls the Exodus tradition found in Ps 77:18-19:

> Thy way was through the sea,
> thy path through the great waters;
> yet thy footprints were unseen.
> Thou didst lead thy people like a flock
> by the hand of Moses and Aaron.

Jesus encounters the crowd the next day and reproaches them for seeking him out not because they "see (understand) the signs," but because their stomachs are full. They should work rather for the "food which endures to eternal life" (v 27). John sets up at this point the tension between faith and works. Typically, the people ask, "What must we do, to be doing the works of God?" Jesus emphasizes the only "work" that God desires, namely, faith in him whom God has sent (v 29).

To substantiate his divine mission, the people demand a

sign from Jesus like the one Moses performed in producing manna in the wilderness. We have already seen how the theme of manna figures significantly in the Exodus/Passover traditions. Jesus corrects the people by saying that it was not Moses who gave them the bread from heaven. Rather, it is his Father who gives the true bread from heaven, which of course is Jesus himself:

> I am the bread of life. Your ancestors ate the manna in the wilderness and they died. This is the bread which comes down from heaven, that one may eat of it and not die. (6:49-50; cf. 6:35-40)

The true "work" involved in attaining life eternal according to Jesus is believing that he is the new spiritual bread sent by his Father (6:40, 47). "The Jews," however, respond to Jesus in the same manner as their ancestors did to Moses in the wilderness just prior to the miracle of manna: they "murmur" against him and his saying (v 41. Cf. Ex 16:2, 7-8). They "see" Jesus and his signs but do not believe (v 36).

"The Jews" are not the only ones who "murmur" at Jesus' words. According to v 61, many of Jesus' own disciples murmur at the seemingly shocking thought of eating Jesus' flesh and drinking his blood. The evangelist, however, has in mind the Christian Eucharist, the new Passover sacrifice which was currently being celebrated in his own first century community. John's focus again is on faith. Jesus acknowledges that some of his disciples do not believe the words spoken to them (v 64). In contrast to these disciples who fall away from Jesus at this point, Peter, speaking for the Twelve, confesses to him: "You have the words of eternal life; and we have believed and have come to know that you are the Holy One of God" (vv 68-69).

The Fourth Evangelist continues, then, to utilize the rich symbolism of the Exodus/Passover in John 6. Through these motifs John communicates that the messianic age has arrived in the person of Jesus. Jesus replaces the person of Moses by feeding the people with the true bread from heaven. Indeed,

Jesus replaces the old manna itself, which was not able to prevent death. As the living bread come down from heaven, Jesus will give eternal life to all who partake of him. One need only believe in his life-giving words.

John anticipates Jesus' third Passover at the conclusion of John 6. Jesus acknowledges a devil in the midst of the Twelve, Judas, the man who will treacherously betray him and bring about his death (vv 70-71). It is to this third Passover at the end of Jesus' earthly ministry that we now turn.

f. The Third Passover: John 13-19

The most significant events that constitute Jesus' last Passover in Jerusalem are his last meal and last discourse with his disciples (John 13-17) and his passion and death (John 18-19). John situates Jesus' two previous Passovers in the Book of Signs where Jesus directs his works and sayings to a wider audience. In view of these signs, this audience then chooses to believe in Jesus or reject him. John places the last Passover significantly in the Book of Glory, which is directed primarily at those who have come to believe in Jesus. We have already seen how John unfolds the theme of faith in our discussion of the first and second Passovers. This theme reaches its fullest exposition in the Book of Glory which begins thus:

> Now before the feast of the Passover, when Jesus knew that his hour had come to depart out of this world to the Father, having loved his own who were in the world, he loved them to the end. (Jn 13:1)

The "hour" of his death, resurrection, and ascension, the most complete manifestation of the Father's glory, has now come. This hour is set during the time of Passover. The mention of the betrayer, Judas Iscariot, in 13:2 links this third and final Passover with the second (6:70-71). Like Judas, those who reject Jesus will soon find him and bring about his dishonorable death. At this Passover, however, Jesus focuses upon those who believe in him by teaching them in an extended discourse the meaning of his "hour" and their own discipleship in faith.

Unlike the Synoptic Gospels, the last supper which the Johannine Jesus shares with his disciples is not the sacrificial Passover meal which is customarily eaten on the 14th of Nisan. John instead schedules the last supper on the evening of the 13th of Nisan, the day *before* the beginning of the Passover celebration (cf. Jn 18:28).

It is most likely that the reasons for John's change of chronology are theological. We recall that the Jews reckon their days from evening to evening. Pilate condemns Jesus at the sixth hour, or noon, of the 13th of Nisan (19:14). Jesus is crucified and left to die during the preparations for the Passover meal which will be celebrated that evening which begins the 14th of Nisan. Jesus' death would thus coincide with the priestly slaughter of the Passover lambs in the temple. For John, Jesus replaces these lambs as the true Lamb of God. The proclamation of John the Baptist at the very outset of Jesus' ministry, "Behold, the Lamb of God, who takes away the sin of the world!" is fulfilled on Golgotha (1:29).

One detects further Passover symbolism in John's account of Jesus' death. Unlike the Synoptics, John records the detail that a sponge full of vinegar is held up to Jesus on a branch of *hyssop* (19:29). Hyssop is used in the Exodus story to sprinkle the doorposts with the blood of the lamb (Ex 12:22). Moreover, only John narrates that Jesus' legs were not broken, fulfilling the Scriptures regarding the Passover lamb that "you shall not break a bone of it" (Ex 12:46). Finally, as the blood of the sacrificed lamb is poured out upon the altar in the temple, so also is Jesus' blood poured out (with water) from his pierced side (19:34).

John's story, however, does not end in death but in life. Jesus rises from the dead and makes his glorious appearances to his followers. Nevertheless, John does not ignore his theme of faith which is so characteristic of his previous Passover accounts and, indeed, his gospel as a whole. The faith demanded of the people and of his disciples is now demanded of us, the reader, as John will write in 20:30-31:

Now Jesus did many other signs in the presence of the disciples, which are not written in this book; but these are written *that you may believe that Jesus is the Christ, the Son of God, and that believing you may have life in his name.*

3

Tabernacles

a. Tabernacles in the Hebrew Bible

The Jewish liturgical calendar contain three major pilgrimage feasts. The first is the one discussed in the previous chapter, the Feast of Unleavened Bread (later joined with the feast of Passover), which the Jews celebrate in the spring at the harvesting of the barley crop. Seven weeks later at the beginning of summer the Feast of Weeks appears, marking the end of the grain season with the harvesting of wheat. The last, held in autumn of the year, is the focus of this chapter, the feast of Tabernacles.

All three feasts were adopted by the Israelites from their ancient near eastern neighbors and were primarily agricultural celebrations at the beginning. However, in the course of their development, all three festivals were "historicized" and associated with a specific event of the great Israelite past: Passover with the Exodus, Weeks with the giving of the Torah, and Tabernacles with the wilderness period of the people.

The feast of Tabernacles is known by different names in the Hebrew Bible: the feast of Ingathering (*'āsîp*) in the earliest liturgical calendars (Ex 23:16 and 34:22) and the feast of Booths (*sukkôt*) in the later liturgical calendars (Dt 16:13, 16; Lev 23:34). The Hebrew *sukkôt* ("booths" or "huts") is rendered in the Vulgate as *tabernacula*, hence the English designation of the feast as Tabernacles. As one of the most important and popular feasts of the calendar, it is sometimes referred to only as "the feast of the Lord" (Lev 23:39; Num 29:12; Judg 21:19) or "the feast" (1 Kings 8:2; Ezek 45:25; Neh 8:14). The two names for Tabernacles highlight dual aspects of the feast. On one hand, the feast of Ingathering is a celebration in thanksgiving for the harvest. On the other hand, the feast of Booths commemorates God's protection of the people as they dwelled in booths during their sojourn in the wilderness. Both of these features are preserved in the single feast of Tabernacles.

The feast of Ingathering was a joyous festival of an agricultural people. Held in the fall, it celebrated the harvesting of grapes and olives that matured in the hot summer sun. The date of the feast at this point was not yet fixed, since the time of harvesting differed from year to year (cf. Ex 23:16; Dt 16:13). It was an occasion of much carousing. Many imbibed in the new wine from the presses of the recently plucked grapes. It was during one such feast that the priest, Eli, mistook Hannah's fervent praying for intoxication (1 Sam 1:14-15). Moreover, dancing was part of the revelries, as we infer from Judg 21:19-23. Here, the Benjaminites carried off the women of Shiloh as they participated in the vineyard dances during "the yearly feast of the Lord at Shiloh" (Judg 21:19. cf. 1 Sam 1:3).

The earliest calendars concluded their injunctions for the three agricultural feasts with the stipulation, "Three times in the year shall all your males appear before the Lord God" (Ex 23:17; 34:23). The feast of Ingathering thus developed into a more formal religious pilgrimage festival from its agricultural origins.

One first encountered the designation of the festival as the feast of Booths (Tabernacles) in the later Deuteronomic liturgical calendar, Dt 16:13. A principal feature of the celebration, these booths were temporary shelters constructed in the vineyard from leafy branches. They provided a second home for harvesters during the picking season, eliminating the need of returning to more permanent abodes at the end of the day. An added feature in the Deuteronomic calendar was the precept that "you shall keep the feast of booths seven days" (v 13). The pilgrimage feast thus became a week long celebration.

One found the most developed prescriptions for the feast in the priestly liturgical calendar, Lev 23:33-36, 39-43. This calendar specified an exact date for the feast: "the 15th day of the seventh month" or the 15th of Tishri (September-October). It stipulated that the first day of the feast be a day of solemn rest. Moreover, it added an eighth day to the feast, also a day of rest, on which the people came together for worship and sacrifice. This day was set apart from the seven days of festivities and functioned as a conclusion for the feast to help the people make the transition back to normal life.

Regarding the seven festal days, Lev 23:40 continued:

> And you shall take on the first day the fruit of goodly trees, branches of palm trees, and boughs of leafy trees, and willows of the brook; and you shall rejoice before the Lord your God seven days.

We see that v 40 preserved the aspect of the feast as a time of rejoicing. Although the purpose of the fruit was not given at this point, the rabbis would take up the matter in their deliberations. The various branches were used to construct the booths housing the people for the duration of the feast. According to a post-exilic text, the people erected these huts on their roofs, in their courtyards, in the courts of the temple, and in the different squares in Jerusalem (Neh 8:16). Not only used to build the huts, the branches were also carried by the worshippers during the feast (2 Macc 10:6-8; Ps 118:27).

Lev 23:42-43 provided an important added dimension to the feast:

> You shall dwell in booths for seven days; all that are native in Israel shall dwell in booths, that your generations may know that I made the people of Israel dwell in booths when I brought them out of the land of Egypt: I am the Lord your God. (cf. Hos 12:10)

For the first time, the feast was associated with a particular period in the salvation history of the people, viz., their time in the wilderness after their dramatic flight from Egypt. Tabernacles thus evolved into an "historicized" feast gathering each generation to "remember" the days when God protected and cared for their ancestors in the wilderness. Although some traditions in the Hebrew Bible regarded the wilderness period as a time of the people's murmuring against God (cf. Ex 16:1-3; 17:1-7), other traditions considered the wilderness era as the idealized period in the God/Israel relationship. According to the prophet Hosea, it was the time of honeymoon between God and his wife, Israel (Hos 2:14-23), the time when God healed and fed the infant Israel, and taught him how to walk (Hos 11:1-4. cf. Dt 32:10-14). These were the images that the people recalled, while living in their huts during the feast of Tabernacles.

By the time of the prophet Zechariah, the feast had acquired eschatological significance. As one of the *haptarah* passages read on the first day of the festival in later times (*t. Meg.* 31a), Zechariah 14 envisioned all the surviving nations going up to Jerusalem to worship God during the feast of Tabernacles (Zech 14:16). Moreover, the prophet warned that if they did not make the pilgrimage, "there will be no rain upon them" (14:17). A prayer for rain could be found earlier in Zech 10:1. Although the theme of rain was not present in our previous texts, it is highly likely that prayers for rainfall had been part and parcel of the ceremony since the earliest times. The autumn feast coincided with the beginning of the rainy season which was sorely needed after the hot summer months.

Earlier in Zechariah 14, the rain motif was connected with the theme of light:

> On that day there shall be neither cold nor frost. And there shall be continuous day (it is known to the Lord), not day and not night, for at evening time there shall be light. On that day living waters shall flow out from Jerusalem, half of them to the eastern sea and half of them to the western sea; it shall continue in summer as in winter.

> And the Lord will become king over all the earth; on that day the Lord will be one and his name one. (Zech 14:6-9)

The theme of light also occurred in Psalm 118, one of the Hallel psalms sung during Tabernacles:

> The Lord is God,
>   and he has given us light.
> Bind the festal procession with branches,
>   up to the horns of the altar! (Ps 118:27)

We note the reference to the leafy boughs that were carried in the festal procession (cf. 2 Macc 10:6-8). The themes of water and light would dominate certain temple rituals of the feast as they were described in the earliest rabbinic codification of Jewish laws, the Mishnah.

b. Tabernacles in the Mishnah

Although the final redaction of the Mishnah occurred some time during the 2nd Century C.E., there is no question that some of its legislation reflected a much earlier period when the temple was still in operation. The laws regarding Tabernacles were handled in tractate *Sukkah*, found in the second division of the Mishnah, *Moed*, which focused on religious feasts. Regulations regarding the construction of the booths and their seven day occupancy during the feast were the topic of *m. Sukk.* 1 and 2.

M. Sukk. 3 and parts of 4 detailed the laws concerning the "four species." On the basis of Lev 23:40, the rabbis named "four species" of plants that had particular cultic significance for Tabernacles. The "fruit of goodly trees," the citron (*etrog*), represented the yield of the harvest. Tied into a bunch called the *lulab* were branches of three different trees: "branches of palm trees" (*lulab*), "boughs of leafy trees," or myrtle branches (*hadasim*), and "willows of the brook," (*arabot*). The "four species" were carried in processions in the temple during the seven days, the citron in the left hand and the *lulab* in the right. While the people processed, they chanted the Hallel

(Psalms 113-118) and would wave the "four species" at the beginning and end of Psalm 118 and during the v 25 of the psalm (*m. Sukk.* 3:9). We already noted the Tabernacles themes of light and branches in Psalm 118 above.

The Mishnah dealt with two other rituals for the feast of Tabernacles that will be of special consequence for our discussion of John 7. First of all, *m. Sukk.* 4:9 mentioned a special water-libation ceremony during the seven days of Tabernacles. This Tabernacles rite was most likely connected with the petitions for rain during the upcoming rainy season. Each day a procession from the temple would make its way down to the pool of Siloam and draw up a golden flagon of water. Journeying back to the temple, the cortege would pass through the Water Gate accompanied by blasts of the *shofar*. The Water Gate had special eschatological significance. R. Eliezer b. Jacob identified it as the south gate envisioned in Ezek 47:1-5 through which waters of life would flow and issue out from under the threshold of the temple (*m. Šeqal.* 6:3, *m. Mid.* 2:6. cf. *t. Sukk.* 3.3-9).

With the golden flagon in hand, a priest would proceed up the ramp to the altar and pour the water into one of the two silver bowls positioned there. These bowls were also mentioned in Zech 14:20. Into the other bowl, the priest would pour a libation of wine. Spouts in each of the two bowls allowed the water and wine to flow out onto the altar. Another rabbinic work, *t. Sukk.* 3.11-12, interpreted the miracle of the water from the rock (Ex 17:1-7, Num 20:8-13) as the ancient prototype of the Tabernacles water ceremony. The rock at Horeb from which the waters gushed forth was described like the Tabernacles water basin from which the ceremonial waters flowed. Moreover, the water from the rock episode was given eschatological importance in *Eccl. Rab.* 1:8:

> As the former redeemer made a well to rise, so will the latter Redeemer bring up water, as it is stated, "And a fountain shall come forth of the house of the Lord, and shall water the valley of Shittim" (Joel 4:18).

M. Sukk. 5:2-4 spoke of the other special ceremony performed during the feast of Tabernacles, viz., the light service. We saw how themes of both water and light were predominant in Zechariah 14. At the end of the first day of the feast, four tall golden candlesticks were set up in the Court of the Women. Atop each candlestick, which could only be reached by ladders, were golden bowls holding oil. Wicks floated in the oil, which were made from the drawers and girdles of the priests. The Mishnah went on to state that, when these wicks were lit, "there was not a courtyard in Jerusalem that did not reflect the light of the House of the Water Drawing."

The illumination represented God's own light. The worshippers would dance before candlesticks accompanied by much singing and playing of instruments. In the ceremony procession toward the eastern entrance to the Court of Women, the priests would turn back towards the temple and proclaim:

> Our ancestors when they were in this place turned with their backs toward the Temple of the Lord and their faces toward the east, and they worshipped the sun toward the east (Ezek 8:16); but as for us, our eyes are turned toward the Lord.

Before we move on to John's treatment of the feast of Tabernacles, we would like to summarize our findings from the Hebrew Bible and the Mishnah. Like the feast of Passover, the feast of Tabernacles underwent a development from an agricultural celebration to an "historicized" one. However, even in its later evolution it never lost its agricultural associations. The occasion of the feast was the autumn harvest of grapes and olives. It derived its name from the custom of constructing booths in the vineyards during this time. The feast evolved into an eight-day pilgrimage observance held at the temple in Jerusalem. By this time, the feast was identified with the wilderness period during which the people lived in booths under God's protective eye. Although a time of joy and thanksgiving, it nevertheless was a time of petition, entreating God to make the rains fall again. The worshippers looked expectantly to a future time when life-giving waters will flow from the temple and invigorate the land, just like water flowed for their ancestors from the rock in the wilderness.

c. Tabernacles in the Gospel of John: Introduction

The feast of Tabernacles provides the backdrop for chapters 7 and 8 of John's gospel. We will bracket for our discussion the story of the adulteress (7:53—8:1-11), a later non-Johannine addition which seems to interrupt the Tabernacles connection between John 7 and 8. John arranges his episodes regarding Jesus in three distinct time periods during the Tabernacles season: before the Tabernacles feast (7:1-13); during the middle of the feast (7:14-36); and on the last day of the feast (7:37-52; 8:12-59). In each particular scene, John throws into relief the speculation and misunderstanding of the Jerusalem population over who Jesus really is.

d. Tabernacles in John: Before the Feast (Jn 7:1-13)

John begins Chapter 7 by relating that Jesus stayed in Galilee and would not go to Judea, "because the Jews sought to kill him" (v 7. cf. 5:16). However, since the feast of Tabernacles was at hand (v 2), and all males were under a religious obligation to make a pilgrimage to Jerusalem at this time, the question of Jesus going to Jerusalem (and possibly being killed) comes to the forefront. His brothers encourage him to go up to the feast and perform his dazzling feats of wonder. John poignantly adds, however, "For even his brothers did not believe in him" (v 5). His own kin see the external "signs," but do not penetrate more deeply into their true significance.

Jesus responds cryptically to their inadequate faith by saying, "My time has not yet come, but your time is always here" (v 6). His brothers assume that Jesus did not think it was the right moment to be in Jerusalem. Jesus, however, is really referring to the "hour" of his death, resurrection, and ascension. This "hour" is reserved for the next feast to come to pass in Jesus' ministry, viz., his third Passover. Jesus does go up to Jerusalem, but in secret. During the feast, "the Jews" (the authorities) search for him, asking around pointedly, "Where is that man?" They propose to catch him and "nail" him, so to speak. The people's reaction underscores the division among them about who Jesus is, some insisting that "he is a good man," others, that "he is leading the people astray" (vv 10-12). However, no one would voice their honest opinion, for fear of retribution by the Jewish authorities.

e. Tabernacles in John: The Middle of the Feast (Jn 7:14-36)

We have examined much of this section in our discussion of Sabbath above. Jesus resumes the Sabbath question that began in John 5 and argues that if circumcision took precedence over the Sabbath, how much more so does the healing of a person's body transcend the Sabbath (vv 21-24). Jesus insists on his divine origins and that he teaches solely under the Father's authority, not of his own (vv 16-18).

His sayings again provoke different reactions that exhibit misunderstandings about Jesus. Some of the people of Jerusalem wonder how a man who has a "warrant on his head" can speak openly in the temple. Furthermore, since they are theologically informed enough to realize that what Jesus says is blasphemous, they wonder if the authorities are actually acknowledging Jesus as the Messiah. Since it is the feast of Tabernacles, these eschatological speculations would not be unfounded. Yet, the existing popular theology of the Christ cautions them that Jesus does not conform to messianic expectations: no one knows where the true Messiah will come from, but everyone knows that Jesus is from Galilee (vv 25-27). Jesus counters that their theological convictions really expose their ignorance of who the Messiah is and from where he comes. Some react to their perception of Jesus' blasphemy by trying to arrest him. Others, in the meantime, believe in him as the Messiah, saying, "when the Christ appears, will he do more signs than this man has done?" Yet, even this camp displays its misconception of Jesus by operating under a model of a wonder-working

Messiah (vv 28-31).

Monitoring the dissension caused by Jesus through informants, the Pharisees and priests decide to send the temple police to arrest him. However, Jesus confounds the police by saying that he will only be around for a little longer. Then, he will return to the one who sent him, and they will seek him in vain. The bewildered Jews wonder if Jesus is going to "skip town." The picture the evangelist paints is the complete and utter mystification of the Jewish masses regarding who Jesus truly is (vv 32-36).

f. Tabernacles in John: The Last Great Day (Jn 7:37—8:59)

The disorder and confusion wrought by Jesus in Jerusalem reaches its climax on the last and great day of the feast of Tabernacles. On the seventh day, the priests pass through the Water Gate and encircle the sacred altar seven times with the waters drawn from the pool of Siloam. Amid the solemnity and pomp of this final libation rite, Jesus stands up in the temple and proclaims:

> If any one thirst, let that one come to me and drink. The one who believes in me, as the scripture has said, "Out of his heart shall flow rivers of living water." (7:38)

The history of exegesis on this particular verse reveals two possible interpretations: that Jesus is the source of the rivers of living water or that the believer is. In good company with many ancient and modern commentators, we prefer the former interpretation which understands Jesus as the wellspring of living water. According to v 39, the water is identified with the Spirit which will be given when Jesus is glorified. Moreover, the Christological interpretation would be consistent with John's overall replacement theology of Jewish feasts and institutions, as we will see shortly.

The verse from the Scriptures to which Jesus refers in v 38 is uncertain. It is not an exact quotation of any passage in either the Hebrew or the Greek texts of the Hebrew Bible. Indeed, the question of the verse's origin bears directly upon the question of the source of living water. We have already discussed several OT texts that are closely connected to the Tabernacles celebration. Zech 14:8 describes "living waters" which shall flow out of Jerusalem "on that day." Rabbinic tradition identifies the Water Gate of the Tabernacles ceremony with the south gate of the temple envisioned in Ezek 47:1-5. From this gate the healing, life-giving waters will pour forth, invigorating the whole region. The rabbis also see in the water-libation rite its prototype in the wilderness miracle of the water from the rock. In the latter age, a redeemer like Moses will bring forth new water from the rock.

If John intends that Jesus is the source of living water, he draws from the rich Jewish background for the feast of Tabernacles. Jesus becomes the new temple from which the waters of life will burst forth. Jesus becomes the new rock in the wilderness that quenches the people's thirst. Jesus invites those who believe in him to satisfy their thirst now with water he provides. The outpouring of water signals that the messianic age has arrived in his own person as the new Moses. John will symbolize this living water in the water which will issue forth with the paschal blood from Jesus' pierced side (Jn 19:34). It is only after Jesus is glorified in his death and resurrection that the Spirit (which the water represents) will be dispatched.

Besides the water imagery from the Tabernacles feast, John also makes use of its light imagery. Jesus replaces the light that radiates from the great candelabra in the Court of Women by proclaiming in that very court: "I am the light of the world; anyone who follows me will not walk in darkness, but will have the light of life" (8:12). Jesus has spoken of the "bread of life (6:25)" and "the rivers of living waters" (7:38). Now he speaks of "the light of life." Whereas the light from the Court of Women brightened all of Jerusalem (*m. Sukk.* 5:3), Jesus is the "light of the world" itself, extending far beyond the confines of Jerusalem.

The metaphor of light accords with John's penchant towards dualist symbols. As life is set against death (3:36), what is above distinct from what is below (8:23), and truth is opposed to lies (8:44-46), so is light pitched against darkness. At the very beginning of his gospel, John asserts that the divine life empowering Jesus was the light of humanity shining in the darkness, a darkness which could not extinguish that light (1:4-5). Those who do what is evil hate the light for fear of exposure, while those who do what is true come to the light that their deeds may be seen (3:19-21). The light shining through Jesus is his Father's own light of life. Jesus is sent into this world to reveal that very light to those who would believe.

Both instances of Jesus' revelation as the "living water" and the "light of the world" provoke controversies among the populace on the last day of the feast, just as these occurred during earlier points of the feast. John points out that "there was a division among the people over him" (7:43) in response to Jesus' revelation as the source of "living water." Some speculate whether Jesus is the prophet "like unto Moses" (cf. Dt. 18:18) who will bring water from the rock like their former Redeemer (cf. *Eccl. Rab.* 1:9). Others claim that Jesus is the Messiah, generating arguments on the origin of the Christ. Some want to arrest Jesus, although the temple police, persuaded by Jesus, refrain from doing so. Dissension flourishes even among the pharisaic camp when Nicodemus argues in Jesus' defense and is repudiated for doing so (9:45-52).

The debate continues with increased hostility as Jesus reveals himself as "the light of the world." John punctuates Jesus' claims to divinity in his use of the divine name "I AM" in several instances in this chapter. Jesus openly proclaims on this solemn festal occasion, "*I AM* the light of the world." He urgently warns his accusers that they will die in their sins, unless they believe that "I AM" (8:24). In frustration and misunderstanding his opponents demand "Who are you?" (8:25), a question that rings through all of the passages we have examined. The point that John makes is that Jesus has told them from the beginning who he was, viz., that he is God's very son, sent for their salvation. When they lift up the Son of man in crucifixion, then they will know that he is "I

AM" who speaks on behalf of the Father (8:28). "The Jews" however cannot bear to believe this, incurring Jesus' condemnation of them as "children of the devil" (8:43-44). At his final attempt to convince them that "before Abraham was, I AM," "the Jews" react to his apparent blasphemy by trying to stone him (8:58-59).

g. Tabernacles in John: Conclusion

As he did with the feasts of Sabbath and Passover, John exploits the rich symbols of the feast of Tabernacles to articulate his own theology of the person of Jesus. Again for John, Jesus replaces Jewish institutions and customs. In the case of Tabernacles, Jesus becomes the new temple from which the "rivers of living water" will flow. He is the new Moses who will bring up water in the wilderness. Replacing the light of Tabernacles in the Jerusalem temple, Jesus becomes "the light of the world." John becomes more forceful in insisting on Jesus' divinity through the "I AM" sayings. Moreover, in the context of this feast John carries his theme of belief vs. unbelief much further, drawing the lines of the opposing camps quite absolutely: those who believe are "of God"; those who refuse to believe "of the devil."

4

Dedication

a. Dedication in 1 and 2 Maccabees

The Feast of Dedication is known in Hebrew as the Feast of Hanukkah. The ancient Jewish historian, Josephus, calls it the Feast of Lights. Today, at the Western Wall in Jerusalem the eight lamps of a great Hanukkah *mĕnôrah*, one for each day of the feast, are lit during Dedication, even as each Jewish household lights its own *ḥănukkîāh*. Unlike the other feasts we have been studying, it is the only celebration not mentioned in the Hebrew Bible. The main sources for its origin are 1 and 2 Maccabees found in the Septuagint (Greek translation of the Hebrew Bible). Another difference from the other Jewish feasts is that Dedication was from the beginning a feast associated with a particular historical event.[19] This eight-day festival beginning on the 25th of Kislev (November-December) commemorates the rededication of the temple in 164 B.C.E. by Judas Maccabeus.

In order to understand the momentous occasion of the temple's rededication, some background history is necessary. This history begins with the great Macedonian ruler, Alexander the Great (356-323 B.C.E.), who conquered most of the known world, in particular, the lands of the Ancient Near East. While basically respecting the various cultures of the defeated lands,

[19]Several scholars have tried to trace the origins of Dedication to pagan festivals such as winter-solstice celebrations, but these have not found common acceptance.

Alexander promoted the Greek or Hellenistic culture throughout in order to unify his empire. This program of Hellenization had a direct impact on the Jewish people, not only those in the Diaspora, but also in Palestine itself. On one hand, the Jews had to integrate many aspects of the Greek culture in order to survive economically and socially. On the other hand, many Jews resisted Hellenism particularly on religious grounds. Greek polytheism conflicted greatly with Jewish monotheism, the belief in only one God.

Alexander's dream of a unified empire collapsed at his own death, when the empire was divided into four kingdoms among his generals. Two powers contended for the control of Palestine: Egypt in the south under the House of Ptolemy and Syria in the north under the House of Seleucus. For about a hundred years, the Ptolemies controlled Palestine. However, in 198 B.C.E. the Seleucids succeeded them through the victories of Antiochus III. This political change did not effect a radical cultural change among the Jews who, though surrounded by Greek culture, retained their traditional heritage for the most part.

The situation shifted, however, when the Seleucid, Antiochus IV, ascended the throne in 175. Antiochus wished to extend his kingdom through a military campaign against his southern rival, Egypt. Part of his strategy included consolidating the diverse constituents of his own kingdom into a united front (cf. 1 Macc 1:41). The most recalcitrant portion of the population were, of course, the Jews who considered themselves the legitimate owners of the land and who tenaciously adhered to their particular religious way of life.

Antiochus, however, found powerful allies in corrupt segments of the Jewish aristocracy and priesthood. This minority Jewish faction warmly greeted Antiochus' intense program of Hellenization. Seeing an opportunity to fill the most influential position in the Jewish nation with a Hellenist, Antiochus deposed the legitimate high priest, Onias III, and "sold" the high priesthood to his brother, Joshua. Joshua in turn changed his name to the Greek, Jason, and undertook the "priestly" task of having a gymnasium, the epitome of

Greek civilization, built in Jerusalem (1 Macc 1:11-13). The sporting events that took place in the gymnasium were just one example, in which many Jewish priests and aristocrats openly expressed contempt for the traditions of their Jewish ancestors. Since athletes participated in the competitions naked, these Jews would mutilate their genitals rather than incur ridicule from their circumcision (1 Macc 1:14-15). Given that circumcision was regarded as a sign of the covenant, this mutilation was apostasy in the worse sense, greatly offending the moral and religious sensibilities of orthodox Jews. The crisis in Judaism during this time, therefore, not only involved conflicts with an oppressive external power, but also internal confrontations among the alienated Jewish classes.

This crisis culminated in 169-167 B.C.E. In order to replenish his treasury whose reserves were severely depleted in his Egyptian campaign, Antiochus sacked the temple in Jerusalem and stripped it of its wealth (1 Macc 1:20-28). Two years later, Apollonius, an emissary of Antiochus, brutally attacked the city on the Sabbath and set up a military fortress that controlled the city. This fortress, called the Akra, was occupied by renegade Jewish Hellenizers and Gentile militia (1 Macc 1:29-35).

In another attempt to homogenize the pluralism that existed in Palestine and exert tighter control, Antiochus, who now called himself "Epiphanes" or "the Manifest (God)," then decreed the national worship of the Greek god, Zeus Olympios. Each of his religious measures was geared to abolish all vestiges of Judaism, so that the people "should forget the law and change all the ordinances" (1 Macc 1:41-50). Persecution of the Jews was rampant and open opposition to the decrees resulted in the death penalty (1 Macc 1:60-64. Cf. 1:56-58). The ultimate outrage against Judaism occurred on the 25th of Kislev in 167 B.C.E. A sacrifice was offered in the temple itself on a pagan altar to Zeus, "the desolating sacrilege," which was built over the sacred altar of holocausts (1 Macc 1:59. Cf. Dan 11:31).

Armed resistance against Antiochus was first enacted by a

Jewish priest, Mattathias of the Hasmonean family, and then finally by his son, Judas Maccabeus. Judas conducted a series of successful battles against the forces of Antiochus and eventually defeated them in 164 B.C.E. (1 Macc 2:1—4:35).

The first matter on Judas' agenda as he entered Jerusalem was the purification of the temple. He and his men tore down the "desolating sacrilege" and erected a new altar of holocausts. They rebuilt and refurnished the sanctuary and the temple interior, as well as uprooted the bushes that sprung up in the temple courts. The new lamps that they installed illuminated the sacred ground once again, signalling the restoration of temple order (1 Macc 4:36-51. cf. 2 Macc 10:1-4). The temple was rededicated on the 25th of Kislev, 164 B.C.E., three years after the defilement of the holy altar by Antiochus. The commemoration of this event came to be known to future generations as the feast of Dedication.

The accounts of the celebration in 1 Macc 4:52-59 and 2 Macc 10:5-8 reveal the similarity that the feast of Dedication has with the feast of Booths/Tabernacles. In fact, 2 Macc 1:9 refers to Dedication as "the feast of Booths in the month of Kislev." In connection with the feast of Booths, 2 Macc 10:6 also explains the celebration by referring to the flight of many Jews to escape the persecution of Antiochus Epiphanes:

> And they celebrated it for eight days with rejoicing, in the manner of the feast of booths, remembering how not long before, during the feast of booths, they had been wandering in the mountains and caves like wild animals. (2 Macc 10:6)

Although there is no mention of living in actual booths, 2 Macc 10:6 recalls the theological rationale for the feast of Booths in Lev 23:42-43, viz., so that Israel may remember God's protection during their wanderings in the wilderness.

If we include Tabernacles' eighth day of solemn assembly (Lev 23:34-36), both feasts were held for eight days. Both were joyous occasions, during which the Hallel was chanted to the accompaniment of musical instruments. During both celebrations, branches and palm fronds were carried and waved in processions. As in the feast of Tabernacles, lights were lit during Hanukkah. A legendary account in 2 Macc 2:18-36 associated the lighting of the lamps with the sacred fire of the temple which was miraculously preserved upon the temple's destruction. It was found later by Nehemiah when the temple was rebuilt (cf. also 2 Macc 1:8). Moreover, 2 Macc 2:9-12 related traditions about how fire from heaven descended and consumed the sacrifice at the dedication of the altar at the time of Moses (cf. Lev 9:24) and at the dedication of the temple during the time of Solomon (cf. 2 Chron 7:1). Later Jewish legal texts prescribed the kindling of lamps in each household, one for each day of the feast.

Significant was the fact that the first temple built by Solomon and the second temple of the post-exilic period were both dedicated during the feast of Tabernacles (1 Kings 8:2, 65; Ezra 3:1-4). In order to dramatize the rededication of the temple after being purified of the desecration by Antiochus, it was very likely that Judas modelled his celebration after the liturgy of Tabernacles. Indeed, 2 Macc 2:8-12 highlighted theologically the continuity of worship in the dedications of Moses' altar, of Solomon's temple, and the newly purified temple during "the feast of Booths in the month of Kislev" (2 Macc 1:9).

The feast of Dedication, therefore, commemorated the rededication of the temple, which was the climax of the persecution, struggle, and ultimate victory of the Jews under Judas Maccabeus against their oppressors. These oppressors, moreover, took on two forms. One was found in the person of Antiochus Epiphanes, the man who sought to bend the will of the Jews towards what they considered as idolatry. On the other hand, the Jews faced an oppressor from within as well as from without. This oppressor was personified in that segment of the Jewish people who should have known better: the Hellenizing priests and aristocracy. These supported Antiochus Epiphanes and strove to sway the people away from the faith of their ancestors. In their apostasy, they represented a far more ruthless and unforgivable opponent to the Jewish people than Antiochus himself.

Imbedded in the festal celebration of Dedication was the very issue of the identity of the Jewish people. It was a people who worshipped only one God and who were bound by Torah. It was a people who worshipped this one God in the one holy sanctuary in Jerusalem, living out lives of Torah in the reality of daily existence. This reality contained the genuine possibility that another Antiochus might set up another "desolating sacrilege" again in their holy place. Also as feasible was the notion that some of their own kind would blaspheme the Holy One of Israel and lead others astray into idolatry. Throughout this joyous celebration lurked the memory of the temple's desecration and the nightmare that it could happen again. The feast of Dedication, therefore, summoned the people to remain steadfast to the law of their God and, by doing so, proclaim, "Never again!"

b. Dedication in John 10:22-42

The last feast that Jesus celebrates in John's gospel before the "hour" of his death and resurrection is the feast of Dedication. Unlike the other feasts we have studied in the Fourth Gospel, the connections between Jesus' discourses and the feast are not so readily apparent. John does not capitalize on the symbolism of light that pervades the feast of Dedication. He had already developed this theme in Jesus' Tabernacles discourses (Jn 8:12). He may have only desired to continue the chronology of feasts and bring his narrative closer to the decisive third Passover. Or, he may have wanted to make a connection between Jesus' Tabernacles discourses and his revelation at Dedication, the feast of Tabernacles in the month of Kislev. John's remark that it was the time of Dedication may have simply been taken from the tradition. The ambience of the feast of Dedication is very suitable for John's purposes, however. Through it, John's underscores the suspicion and unbelief of "the Jews" when confronted with Jesus as both Messiah and Son of God.

Jesus had remained in the hostile city of Jerusalem since the feast of Tabernacles and had cured the blind man at the pool of Siloam on the Sabbath (9:1-40). The animosity that the Jewish leaders felt towards Jesus at Tabernacles becomes even greater as they perceive Jesus transgressing the Sabbath. Jesus fans the flames even further as he censures pharisaic leadership in his shepherd and sheepgate discourses (10:1-22). John will take up this shepherd theme in Jesus' Dedication discourse (10:25-29).

John begins the narrative in 10:22 with three details: that it was the feast of the Dedication at Jerusalem, that it was winter, and that Jesus was walking in the temple's portico of Solomon. The detail that "it was winter" refers to the month of December, during which the feast of Dedication occurs. Since the feast of Dedication commemorates the rededication of the temple, it is quite appropriate for John that the confrontation between Jesus and "the Jews" occurs in the temple precincts. The oldest colonnade on the eastern face of the temple, Solomon's Portico offered protection during the winter against the harsh wind. It was a fitting gathering place when "the Jews" demanded of Jesus: "How long will you keep us in suspense? If you are the Christ, tell us plainly" (10:24).

Popular speculations regarding Jesus' messiahship filled the air during the feast of Tabernacles months before (7:25-27, 31, 41-42). The encounter between the Jews and Jesus now during Dedication is similar to the question asked of Jesus during his trial before the Sanhedrin in Lk 22:67: "'If you are the Christ, tell us.' But he said to them, 'If I tell you, you will not believe.'" The Johannine Jesus replies, "I told you, and you do not believe" (10:25). Nowhere in John does Jesus actually claim to be the Messiah, because, as we have seen in our discussion of Tabernacles, Jesus does not conform to popular views of the Messiah and his coming.

Yet, for John, Jesus is the Messiah, a fact witnessed by the works that Jesus performs in his Father's name (10:25). Nevertheless, even in the face of these extraordinary signs, "the Jews" do not believe. They do not belong to his sheep. His own sheep would recognize his voice and follow him (10:25-26). John's introduction of the sheep imagery here subtly reinforces Jesus' messiahship. The Messiah was believed to be a descendant of the House of David, the great Israelite king who began his career as a shepherd (1 Sam 16:11; 17:34-36). Unlike the Davidic Messiah, however, Jesus as Messiah offers his sheep the possibility of eternal life: "No one shall snatch them out of my hand" (10:28). From the perspective of the Johannine community, "the Jews" who do not believe in Jesus are cast in the role of "wolves" who snatch and scatter the unprotected flock (10:12). It is these "Jews" who try to thwart the salvation of the people by their unbelief.

Jesus' messiahship is of another sort than that held by popular opinion. Jesus is Messiah precisely because he is God's son. His own Father has delivered the sheep into his care and protection. It is the Father's power entrusted in him that keeps the sheep from being snatched by the wolves. The movement of Jesus' discourse climaxes in his unimpeachable claim: "I and the Father are one" (10:30).

Recalling the purpose of the feast of Dedication and the feelings surrounding it, we try to imagine the effect of Jesus' words on his Jewish audience. In the background of the feast is the constant reminder of the temple's desecration by Antiochus Epiphanes, the one who had instituted the false worship of an alien god. At stake is the identity of the Jewish people who venerate the one God of Israel, particularly through their rigorous adherence to Torah. This Torah forbids the worship of any other god beside Yahweh (Ex 20:3). Here before "the Jews" in their holy temple is someone claiming to be God's own son, united with the Father in power and authority. From the Jews' perspective, this declaration is blasphemy. It threatens to defile the sacred ground a second time. Reacting accordingly, the Jews take up stones to rid the community of this blasphemer (10:31).

Jesus responds boldly to their attempt on his life. He points out that he performed "many good works from the Father" (10:31). If Jesus truly blasphemed God, he would not have been able to work these signs. His works indeed reveal the truth of his words: that he and the Father are one.

For John, however, "the Jews" persist in their unbelief. They articulate openly what they feel in their heart: "We stone you for no good work but for blasphemy; because you, being a man, make yourself God" (10:33). The issue for John is Christological. The Jews stubbornly refuse to accept Jesus as Messiah and God's son, even in the face of Jesus' signs. They view Jesus not only as a mere human being, but also a dangerous one in arrogating to himself divinity and influencing others to believe in him.

In answering the Jews' objections, Jesus utilizes the rabbinic hermeneutical principle, which we had encountered in his second Sabbath controversy (7:23). Through an *a minori ad maius* (lesser to greater) argument, Jesus maintains that if in the Scriptures which cannot be nullified, those who receive and treasure the word of God are called "gods" (cf. Ps 82:6), how much more should the one who reveals God's very word describe himself as Son of God (10:34-36)? The depiction of himself as the one "whom the Father consecrated" would not be lost on his Jewish audience as they celebrate the feast of Dedication (10:36). We saw that the feast recalled a series of temple dedications from Moses, to Solomon, to Judas Maccabeus. For John, Jesus replaces the temple as the Holy One truly consecrated by God.

In 10:37 the Johannine Jesus returns again to the theme of faith and works, a theme that has run through all his other festival discourses. Jesus argues,

> If I am not doing the works of my Father, then do not believe me; but if I do them, even though you do not believe me, believe the works, that you may know and understand that the Father is in me and I am in the Father. (10:37-38)

If he himself is unbelievable as the Son consecrated by God, Jesus enjoins them to believe in his works that reveal that "the Father is in me and I am in the Father." "The Jews," however, remain unchanged in their opinion of Jesus. They seek to arrest him for his blasphemy, but he escapes from their hands (10:39).

John does not end the scene on a pessimistic note. He describes Jesus leaving Jerusalem and its malevolence to the other side of the Jordan. There Jesus remains in the place where John the Baptist first baptized. The evangelist thereby relates Jesus' messianic revelation in Jerusalem with the beginning of his gospel and the Baptist's denial that he is the Messiah (1:20, 24). It is John at the beginning of Jesus' ministry who had seen and borne witness "that this is the Son of God" (1:34). What is not possible in Jerusalem is now possible across the Jordan. The evangelist concludes his story of Jesus during the feast of Dedication on a theme which has become familiar to us in our discussion of Jewish feasts and John's gospel. He notes the faith that was inspired by Jesus in those who lived across the Jordan:

> Many came to (Jesus) and they said, "John did no sign, but everything that John said about this man was true." *And many believed in him there.* (Jn 10:41-42)

SELECT BIBLIOGRAPHY

Barrett, C.K. *The Gospel According to St. John.* Philadelphia: Westminster, 1978, 2nd ed.

Bloch, Abraham P. *The Biblical and Historical Background of Jewish Customs and Ceremonies.* New York: Ktav, 1980.

Brown, Raymond E. *The Gospel According to John.* AB 29 and 29A; Garden City: Doubleday, 1966 and 1970, Vol. 1 & 2.

de Vaux, Roland. *Ancient Israel: Religious Institutions.* New York: McGraw-Hill, 1965, Vol. 2.

Gaster, Theodore H. *Festivals of the Jewish Year.* New York: Morrow Quill, 1953, 1978.

Kysar, Robert. *John the Maverick Gospel.* Atlanta: John Knox, 1976.

MacRae, George. "The Meaning and Evolution of the Feast of Tabernacles," *CBQ* 22 (1960) 251-276.

Rankin, O.S. *The Origins of the Festival of Hanukkah.* Edinburgh: T & T Clark, 1930.

Saldarini, Anthony J. *Jesus and Passover.* New York: Paulist, 1984.

Segal, J. B. *The Hebrew Passover from the Earliest Times to A.D. 70.* London: Oxford University, 1970.

Schnackenburg, Rudolf. *The Gospel According to John.* New York: Herder & Herder/Seabury/Crossroad, 1968, 1980, 1982, Vol. 1-3.

Strand, Kenneth A., ed. *The Sabbath in Scripture and History.* Washington: Review and Herald Publ. Asso., 1982.

Notes

Notes